The Complete Book of
FLOORING

The Complete Book of
FLOORING

Laurie Williamson

The Crowood Press

First published in 2004 by
The Crowood Press Ltd
Ramsbury, Marlborough
Wiltshire SN8 2HR

www.crowood.com

British Library Cataloguing-in-Publication Data
A catalogue record for this book is available from the British Library.

ISBN 1 86126 657 X

Typeset and designed by Naomi Lunn

Printed and bound by Craft Print International Ltd, Singapore

690.16

CONTENTS

INTRODUCTION

Of course, for most of us, the ultimate aim is successfully to create a sense of space and ostentation within the context of existing surroundings, and the right choice of flooring and floor covering is the best way we can start to achieve this. Whether we are maintaining a sense of time and period applicable to older properties or simply making a statement of our beliefs and origins within modern surroundings, the floor area is the palette from which all our expressions will emanate. Even the passage of time and the variety of locations have hardly dimmed the drive towards reflecting where we live, our climate, and even our status. And to achieve these goals suc-cessfully, a level of knowledge about the floor structure and the impact the floor surroundings, including heat and light, will have on your choice of floor cover-ing is essential.

The *Complete Book of Flooring* will help you do this by considering the huge variety of options available within the context of prevailing conditions. For centuries now, from the time man first lived on a mud floor that he covered selectively with animal skins and rush mats, it seems very little has changed. Of course, the floor surface of today has become far more sophisticated, but inevitably the aims of the floor covering remain the same.

1 ABOUT FLOORS

The wide choice of flooring materials that are available today is truly inspiring, and offers the home owner an ever-widening selection of brand names, styles and product types to choose from. Manufacturers have not been slow to recognize this growing market, where efforts to improve their product designs and to follow trends has resulted in a wide range of good quality materials that are attractive, durable, easier to install and easier to maintain.

In with the old and in with the new appears to be where the demand for stylish good quality flooring is heading, where the progress seen over decades and even centuries with building structures, furnishings and furniture has continued steadily. Yet even with the increasing use of synthetic materials, the tried and tested floor coverings used by our predecessors, such as wood and wool, clearly remain the commonest and most popular choice. Thankfully the UK has also gained from materials imported from its European neighbours and Far Eastern traders. These materials include

A warm wooden floor covering.

Farmhouse slate.

7

natural fibres, grasses, stone and terracotta, and add a superb diversity of choice, the type of diversity that encourages competition and improves product quality, while offering the widest possible selection.

The role of the manufacturer in improving and developing the range of floor coverings available to the general public, while keeping within set boundaries, has had to be twofold. Firstly, in recognizing there was a need for a product range able to move with the times, they then had to make sure it remained attractive, hard-wearing, and suitable to cope with the diversity of climates in the UK. And secondly, and more importantly, they had to cope with the demands placed upon it by the environmentalists.

Of course, all flooring products used by our predecessors were based on natural products, when availability and damage to the environment were not key issues, and where some were more readily available than others. Grasses and wool were, and still are, used extensively as an available floor covering that causes no harm to the local environment. Of course, not all flooring products are so easily recycled. Hardwoods in rainforests have, over time and as a result of excessive demand, reached levels of extreme danger as a direct result of over-

Slate mining in Cornwall.

harvesting. Now, following pressure from environmental groups, extreme measures have been taken to reverse this trend and to protect endangered species.

To meet increased demand created by a reduction in available natural fibres, and to improve product longevity, the number of synthetics and man-made fibres have increased and improved during the last century; but natural products, being well tested, tried and trusted, have always seemed to hold sway. Of course, it has helped matters that natural grasses, coir and wool are easily replicated and readily available, whereas wooden flooring, in all its forms, has undergone quite a transformation. Again this development is largely as a result of pressure from the 'green' groups who have forced manufacturers to revue their policies, resulting in a dramatic increase in laminated and veneered flooring sheets where the look of wood can be reproduced without there being any devastating effect on distant rainforests.

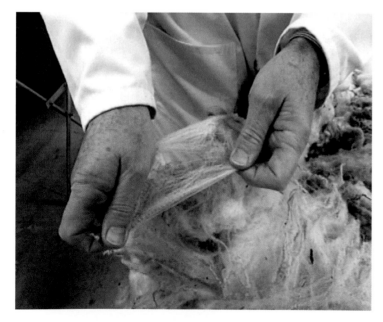

Checking the wool for suitability.

Harvesting grass and wool was clearly an easier option than harvesting trees, so as demand grew for more and more natural flooring products, something had to 'give'. And I think the result must clearly be registered as a resounding success for the manufacturers. As if pressure from the environmentalists was not enough, the building regulators, themselves under pressure to reduce noise levels and energy losses, turned to the flooring manufacturers for help. The result is an improvement in the design and installation techniques of all flooring products, with the insulation levels of both ground-supported and suspended floors also improved.

However, this improvement in the production of man-made or natural floor-covering ranges is only half the answer. Each individual product has its place, as long as it is among the best there is available, and is able to strengthen the drive for suitable and even diverse floor coverings created by interior designers. The introduction of deep and obscure colours, creative and subdued designs, a texture representative of each room and a durability suitable for modern living, have all conjoined to work together and to create what must be considered the intended result. Bare floorboards highly polished and covered with rugs, wall-to-wall carpeting, terracotta tiles and finished marble flooring are just a glimpse of the possibilities now available to create the room of your choice. The improvement in available products has continued to grow at a significant rate, and it must be accepted that no other era can begin to boast such an extensive range of floor-covering possibilities while working so closely with the environment.

A child-friendly bedroom selection.

About Floors

Of course, hard flooring materials are nearly always permanent, and these will form an integral part of any building fabric. Materials such as ceramic tiles, marble, slate and terracotta all fit neatly into the 'hard flooring' category, and each may produce a finished floor of immense and individual beauty. But there is a price to pay for this unquestionable beauty, since structural limitations can restrict installation as hard floors are extremely heavy, and they must be laid upon solid and secure sub-floor foundations. Timber floors, at any level, may require additional reinforcement to enable them to comfortably support the extra load being placed upon them. And, significantly, hard floors are not at all resilient, and have many drawbacks. For instance, anything dropped on them is likely to break, and if a very heavy object is dropped on the floor it could easily damage the floor's surface, requiring expensive restoration. They are cold to the touch, which

Jute carpets, natural flooring.

can be an advantage in hot weather, but a disadvantage in cold, and it is well known that walking or standing on a hard floor for a lengthy period of time can also be extremely tiring.

Clean and fit lines.

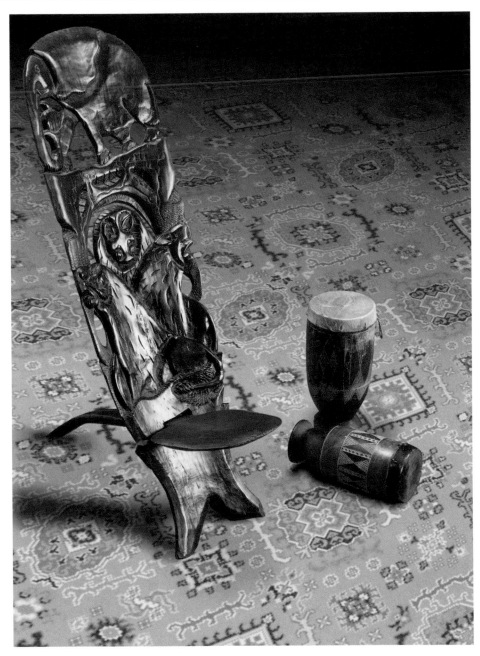

Antique Splendour
Honeysuckle.

A more resilient flooring material, though not quite so hard-wearing as a hard floor, is wooden flooring. This is a truly elegant material, with tongued and grooved 'boards' now demonstrating an evenness that carpenters found very difficult to achieve when they installed the original 'butt-jointed' floorboards in Victorian homes, because these would inevitably shrink and twist as a result of atmospheric changes. Another quality true of wooden floors is that they produce a warm surface that can easily be stained and sealed to a colour of choice — though the dwindling availability of various hardwoods has restricted choice. Fortunately, in more recent years this type of flooring has taken on a new lease of life thanks to the introduction of laminated flooring strips. These 'strips' have been designed to replicate, and indeed provide a very adequate imitation of the 'old-fashioned' – and very expensive – floorboards, parquet flooring and wood-strip boards. Laminated flooring strips are also tongued and grooved to ensure evenness, and they produce a very warm and welcoming surface suitable for almost any room.

More durable and environmentally friendly among the range of manufactured flooring materials are linoleum sheet and cork tiles. This type of material was extremely popular a few decades ago, and they have now improved in resilience and comfort, and can boast a range of colours and styles almost beyond recognition. As well as the improvements in colours, this surface has acquired a cushion backing that is durable while still comfortable to walk on, and is virtually maintenance free. With a new and tougher surface, plus an authentic-looking range of imitations

including marble, slate and wood, this less expensive flooring material is still used very extensively in areas where protection against daily wear and tear is a priority.

And last, but definitely not the least, probably the most popular choice in modern households today is softer flooring materials. These include carpets of pure wool and synthetic fibres, oriental rugs, and a wide range of tried and trusted natural grasses. Much more likely to be considered as a furnishing than a floor covering, carpets and rugs are available in an incredibly wide range of textures, colours and designs.

So in the final analysis, when we look at every aspect of all the floor coverings currently available, and research their historical background, we must conclude that, in agreement with those immortal words uttered by Sir Harold Macmillan, we have indeed 'never had it so good'.

2 FLOOR CONSTRUCTION

Floor construction for domestic dwellings in the UK will normally fall into one of two distinct categories: ground-supported concrete floors; and suspended, beam and block or timber-joist floors. Probably the more common is the ground-supported concrete floor, though because uncontaminated, level and moisture-free building plots are increasingly hard to find, the suspended floor is rapidly growing in popularity.

In both cases the construction process will be similar in that the floor area will first be levelled between the perimeter walls of the house. It will then be stripped of all vegetative materials, ensuring that all topsoil and perishables such as wood and roots are removed, leaving the new floor area cleared and ready to receive a hardcore base. The latter will be laid in layers of 100–150mm, with each layer compacted using a heavy-duty compactor, and the whole base should not exceed 600mm in depth. Old broken bricks, roof tiles and similar dry non-perishable building waste are often used for a hardcore base; it is important that all sizeable air pockets are removed.

Suspended timber first-floor joists.

Ground-supported concrete floors.

Floor Construction

After the hardcore is laid and compacted it will be 'blinded' with a layer of soft sand: this is to prevent any sharp pieces of hardcore puncturing the damp-proof membrane that will now be laid on top of the sand. It is important to note that the Building Regulations specify that measures must be taken to reduce the likelihood of heat loss through this solid concrete floor, so at this stage a layer of insulation can be included to combat this loss of energy.

To prevent dampness rising through the ground and damaging both the floor area and the floor covering, a damp-proof membrane will be installed. This membrane must span from wall to wall, and provide a continuous protective barrier against rising dampness. When the membrane is securely in place, and the insulation if required, the concrete oversite can be laid: at this stage every effort must be made to avoid puncturing the membrane itself, which would almost certainly result in problems at a later date. This building method is common with both ground-supported concrete floors and suspended floors; but from this point on, methods change.

In the former, where the base is stable and free from the risk of rising dampness, the floor will be finished off with either a sand-and-cement screed finish, or a 'floating' chipboard finish, known as a floating floor. However, where the hard-

core base has been built up due to the sloping irregularities of the building site, or where the ground is likely to be contaminated, or there is a distinct risk from rising dampness, then a suspended floor will be used.

Until recently, a suspended floor at both ground and first-floor level would be constructed from softwood timber joists supported by perimeter and intermediate walls. However, the introduction of beam-and-block floors has transformed floor construction, so that builders and developers can cope easily with what used to be problem areas.

Chipboard flooring at first-floor level.

Double joist for added support.

The base for a suspended timber floor is laid in the same way as for a beam-and-block floor, incorporating a damp-proof membrane and leaving a void for ventilation. A suspended timber floor will be constructed from softwood timber joists of a size determined by span and load-bearing requirements. The joists will each be supported by perimeter and intermediate load-bearing walls.

sleeper walls to reduce the overall span of the joists. In the void beneath the suspended floor there will be a risk of damage to the new floor from dry rot and other airborne fungi.

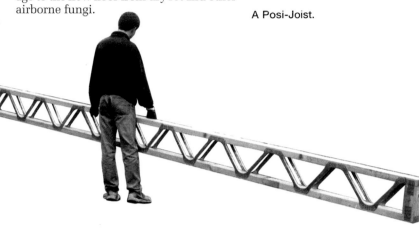

A Posi-Joist.

SUSPENDED TIMBER FLOORING

A suspended timber floor will be constructed from timber joists at both ground-floor and first-floor level. At ground-floor level the timbers will be suspended above the concrete oversite, resting on the perimeter load-bearing walls, and on intermediate, brick-built

(below) The advantages of a Posi-Joist system.

Floor Construction

To combat this, a series of airbricks will be built into the perimeter walls to provide ventilation and encourage a free flow of air. Obviously the airbricks must be kept clear from obstruction at all times. At first-floor level the joists will also be supported by both the perimeter walls, and with internal load-bearing walls, designed and located to provide additional support where required.

To determine the load placed on a floor, Building Regulations have devised a loading table for timber floor joists in domestic dwellings, calculated in kilograms per square metre. The distance between load-bearing supports will determine the size of the joist required to 'carry' the load likely to be imposed upon it. Another determining factor will be the number of joists required, and their spacing, or centres: the wider the spacing or centre, the stronger the joists will need to be. There are three common grades of timber used for this type of construction: General Stress grade (GS), Special Stress grade (SS) and Machine General Stress grade (MGS). The GS and SS grades are assessed visually, noting the grain and the position of knots in the timber, whereas the MGS grade joists are assessed mechanically. By changing the dimension and centres of the floor joists there may be several options to consider. When the joists are in place and secured, the insulation and a floor covering can then be added.

Softwood floorboards are tongued and grooved, and are generally available in widths of up to and exceeding 150mm. These boards will be secured at right angles to the joists using proper flooring nails, with any joins formed directly above a floor joist, for strength. To allow for movement, avoid dampness and permit air flow, a gap will be left around the perimeter walls. This will be concealed when the wall is plastered and skirting boards are fitted. The floorboards, when stained and sealed, will be suitable as a finished floor covering; however, where sheet coverings such as chipboard are used, these are unlikely to be used as a finished floor. This latter form of sheet covering can cover a floor area very quickly, and is now widely used in the building industry; with tongued-and-grooved edges, these boards can provide maximum strength to the flooring covering. Carpets, floor tiles and so on, can be added when construction is complete.

A suspended floor system.

Laying the new 'Jamera' floor system.

This concept has been used in Scandinavia for decades.

Minimum bearing of 90mm required.

Energy conservation is nowadays extremely high on the list of priorities in building construction and design, so any floor area attracts its fair share of attention. Energy can be lost through ground floors, so a layer of insulation material will be added during the construction process to increase the 'u' values of the floor. Where the floor is at a higher level, then noise pollution will be high on the list of considerations. In these instances, and where the floor construction is likely to be a choice of timber floorboards or sheet coverings in chipboard or plywood, insulation can be added either in the floor, or below or above it, and extra care taken with the final floor covering.

BEAM-AND-BLOCK FLOORS

Beam-and-block floors span perimeter walls in the same way as timber joists, but they are manufactured off site, precast from concrete and reinforced by steel bars running though them. Before installation the manufacturer will consult the drawings, and from the foundation layout will determine the length of each beam and produce a detailed drawing showing their finished position. Generally the beams are positioned to accommodate a standard size wall block laid between them. The one significant advantage that beam-and-block floors

Beam-and-block flooring.

Using aircrete blocks for the floor.

have over ground-supported concrete floors is that they save time, in that you do not have to wait for the floor to set.

BEAM-AND-BLOCK FLOORING

Beam-and-block flooring systems have a number of advantages over other forms of floor construction:
- Dry construction shortens the building time.
- Delays due to bad weather are minimized.
- Speed of installation.
- Reduced heat loss through the floor.
- Reduces noise transmission between floors.

A finished floor ready for the joints to be grouted.

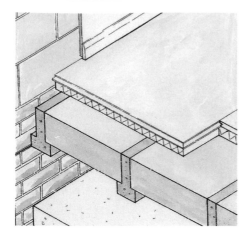

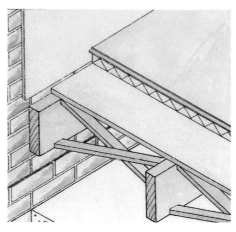

Fig 1 *(far left)*
Insulating a beam-and-block floor.

Fig 2 *(left)*
Insulating a suspended ground floor.

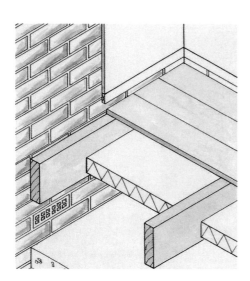

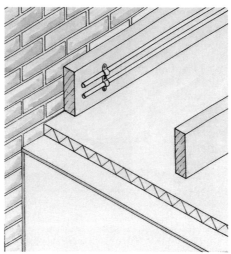

Fig 3 *(far left)*
Insulation suspended between the joists.

Fig 4 *(left)*
Adding upper floor insulation.

As soon as the beams are in place, the concrete blocks can be laid, and a solid, secure base is immediately in place providing a secure working platform; this is certainly an advantage when compared with suspended timber floor construction.

Between these structural beams, aggregate or aircrete blocks will be laid, and any floor insulation will be located between the beam-and-block floor and the finished floor surface.

A FLOATING FLOOR

The term 'floating' has been used to identify floors where the finished floor surface area is not secured – at least, not in a major way – to the floor base area. A floating floor can be a concrete screed, or it can be chipboard sheets. The construction methods are similar to ground-bearing concrete floors and suspended beam-and-block floors in that the base is rigid. A layer of rigid insulation is then added, with the finished floor surface laid on top of the insulation. This gives the impression of the floor surface 'floating' above the rigid concrete base.

FLOOR INSULATION

Building Regulations are particularly stringent when it comes to preventing heat loss through solid or timber floors. New and existing regulations will

Fig 5

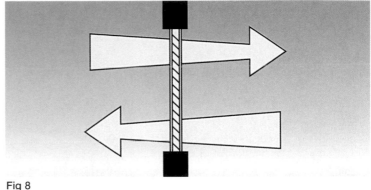

Fig 8

Fig 6

Fig 9

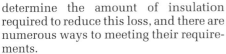

Fig 7

Fig 5
Secure the acoustic
barrier to the sub-floor.

Fig 6
Fit snugly into corners.

Fig 7
Stagger the joints of
acoustic sheeting.

Fig 8
Sound reduction through
floors and walls.

Fig 9
Complete sound barrier.

determine the amount of insulation required to reduce this loss, and there are numerous ways to meeting their requirements.

Where the floor area is a ground-supported concrete floor, a layer of insulation, of a thickness suitable to meet regulation requirements, can be installed. The insulation can be installed between the oversite and the concrete slab, between the concrete slab and the floor screed, and with a 'floating' floor, between the concrete slab and the finished floor surface.

Where the floor is a suspended timber floor the floor insulation can be fitted between the floor joists using proprietary fixings.

Where the floor is a beam-and-block floor, the blocks used to form the floor surface can be of a thermal efficiency to meet the Building Regulations.

NOISE

In all forms of domestic construction, noise is a pollutant requiring significant attention. At ground level noise reduction will be achieved with insulation, but at upper floor levels extra care should be taken in construction. Timber floors are a particular cause for concern where sound transmission is difficult to eradicate, but preventative measures can be taken. The void between the upper floor and the lower ceiling can be filled with a suitable insulation filler. In these instances extra care must be taken to check for electricity cables and water pipes. Another preventative measure will be to install an 'acoustic' strip between the floor surface and the timber joists. Similarly an acoustic strip can be added around the perimeter walls of each room, again reducing sound transmission.

Where the floor surface is already in place, adding this type of noise reduction system can be costly. An alternative would be the inclusion of an acoustic floor covering that can be laid on top of the existing floor surface before the finished floor covering is added. There will be a small reduction in room height, and doors may require adjustments.

AIRBRICKS AND VENTILATION

To prevent dry rot and other airborne fungi causing damage to wooden floors, and to allow good air flow beneath beam-and-block floors, ventilation must be provided by way of a continuous flow of free air beneath the suspended floor. For this purpose airbricks will be built into the perimeter walls of the building at strategic intervals. The airbricks must be kept clear at all times, and although usually added below the damp-proof course, they must remain above ground level.

FLOOR SCREED

A floor screed is a sand and cement mixture laid to provide a flat and smooth floor finish, and is commonly used in domestic building construction. This method of construction – comprising a hardcore base, concrete slab, damp-proof membrane and finished off with a floor screed – has almost completely elimi-

Hire a power trowel for a smooth finish.

nated the risk of dry rot and other fungal damage previously attributed to timber floors. A layer of insulation can be installed between the concrete slab and the floor screed to ensure that it meets with Building Regulation requirements.

A floor screed is a mixture of sharp sand and cement to a ratio of between 1 in 3 and 1 in 4, depending on the depth of the screed. Where the floor is a floating floor the screed will be laid directly on top of the insulation slab. Where there is underfloor heating incorporated into the floor screed, significant time must be allowed for the drying-out process before the underfloor heating is used, to prevent abnormal shrinkage and cracking of the screed. This time zone will also apply where a finished floor surface, including rigid floor tiles, is laid on the screed floor.

3 FLOOR PREPARATION

Before laying a new floor covering, preparations will need to be made to ensure you can achieve the best possible finish. Laying a new floor covering on a new floor reduces the risk of unknown problem areas, but when existing floor coverings are being replaced it is important to take the opportunity to check the base floor area properly. Check an old concrete floor for cracks and erosion, and an old wooden floor for twisting and lifting. If there are loose and damaged floorboards, this is the time either to secure them properly, get them repaired, or to replace them. In the same way that a room is prepared for painting and decorating, so restoring a floor area needs similar consideration and preparation, and in some cases, this may take even longer than laying the actual floor; however, it is the preparation that will yield the results you require. However much you spend on the floor covering, the end result could easily be ruined by shoddy preparations.

Whether you are laying a carpet yourself, or employing a carpet fitter, then the room concerned will need to be cleared of all moveable obstructions, and the base surface checked to ensure that it is in the right condition for the carpet to be laid. In this instance the preparations may not be too tricky or time-consuming, since carpet can be laid on almost any floor surface as long as it is clean and relatively smooth. If it is an old floor that was previously carpeted, you will know if there are any points of unevenness, and this is a good time to deal with any loose and squeaky floorboards, and to remove any unwanted protrusions.

When employing a carpet fitter to carry out the work, try to make sure that the floor is ready for the carpet to be laid. Where additional work is required to the under-floor then the fitter may be prepared to carry this out, but there may be an extra charge.

Fast-track screeding for poor floors.

On a more serious note, where there is evidence of damage through damp or even infestation, carefully check the floor area, removing suspect boards so that the supporting structure can be checked. Where problems are discovered, then solutions must be found before the new floor is laid. When the floor is new, it may be a good idea to go over the area with a straight-edged piece of timber to check for uneven areas. Of course, making good any faults in a floor must be done before the floor covering is laid.

Laying a hard floor or a wooden strip floor is more difficult and requires a much higher level of preparation. Decorative mouldings such as skirting boards, door stops and architraves will need to be removed from around the perimeter walls and the doors so the new flooring can be laid tight to the walls, and in the case of wooden strip floors, to allow for movement. The mouldings can be refitted or replaced to provide a clean, straight edge around the room. Where the finished new surface will be higher than the original, the doors will also need to be removed so they can be planed down until they have enough clearance to open over the new floor level without scraping.

SKIRTING BOARDS AND ARCHITRAVES

Skirting boards, door stops and architraves are typical mouldings popular in all homes, and they provide that extra decorative finishing touch to a floor. In some circumstances these mouldings can remain in situ – for example, when a new carpet is being laid – but in others their removal is a necessity. Care when removing them will help to ensure their future use, and will reduce the risk of damage to walls and plaster.

Before removing skirting boards, always check how they are secured to the wall: in the majority of cases they will simply be nailed at up to 4ft (1.2m) intervals; by looking closely you may find the exact nail positions, and this will help the task of prising the skirting board away from the wall. Note, however, that sometimes the boards may be screwed

Isolator membrane under the carpet.

Isolator membrane covering contaminated sub-floor.

Vinyl and linoleum floor coverings can be bonded to the membrane.

and plugged, and in this case prising them away from the wall could create a lot of surface damage.

The best way to tell whether the skirting is nailed or screwed is the mark at the point of connection: where the mark is irregular it is likely to be a nail, and where it is circular, a screw. By looking closely at the skirting board you should be able to determine the fixing used. Where the boards are screwed on, the screw head will be covered with a small amount of filler; scrape this away, and you should uncover the screw head, and the screw can then be removed using a screwdriver. Although it may well be a little time-consuming, it will keep damage to the wall to an absolute minimum. Of course, when reusing skirting boards the existing holes in the wall cannot be used again because the boards will be relocated in a slightly higher position.

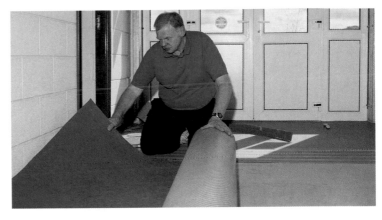

A loose lay system allows for easy removal.

CARPET

Removing old carpet should be a fairly straightforward procedure. Where the carpet is to be relocated and reused, care must be taken not to damage it. Where the carpet is to be discarded, you can cut around the secured areas such as door thresholds to relieve tension and to avoid damage to the threshold strips or the gripper strips as you pull the carpet away.

In some instances carpet is secured around the perimeter with double-sided tape and even tacks, but the most secure method is to use gripper strips. These can be nailed or glued around the perimeter right up to the base of the skirting boards, though not actually touching them. When the old carpet is removed, first check that the gripper strips are secure and unbroken. Next, inspect the floor for dampness and unevenness, and where there are signs of a problem, these areas should be fully researched and treated as necessary.

Carpet, and in particular foam-backed carpet, should not be laid on top of old carpet, because this creates conditions where mildew and damp can thrive.

Suitable for use over damp surfaces.

VINYL TILES

Vinyl tiles can provide a suitable base for other flooring materials, and need not be removed in all cases, providing they are clean and secure. If there is no moisture damage, suggesting a more deep-seated problem, then the wise option may be to leave the vinyl floor in situ – even if a few tiles do need securing – as long as the manufacturer of the new flooring material agrees.

The alternative is to clear the floor surface of all previous coverings and take it back to its original state, which may at least avoid building in problems. To remove vinyl tiles, and because they are generally approximately 12sq in (77sq cm) each, should not be problematic. Using a scraper, prise the tiles free around the edges, and peel them back; keep the scraper at a low angle to reduce the risk of damaging the existing floor surface. Where vinyl tiles are stubborn, the use of a heat gun may be required.

When all the tiles have been taken up, go over the floor carefully to remove all small lumps and bumps; these will certainly show up when a new vinyl or linoleum floor is laid, and could easily damage its surface.

CERAMIC TILES

Removing and replacing a ceramic tile floor covering can be a considerable task, and the age of the floor may well determine how big a task, because older floor tiles can become quite firmly attached to the sub-floor. However, before attempting

Trowel in the smaller cracks.

Repairing a damaged concrete floor.

Warning: Old vinyl-type flooring sheets manufactured before 1986 may contain asbestos fibres, and these are extremely hazardous. When in doubt, contact your Local Authority for advice and information about secure removal. Do not remove or sand this type of surface until you are sure it is safe to do so. It may be possible to lay the new floor covering on top of this material as the best option.

to remove them, first evaluate the floor construction. Where ceramic tiles are secured to a concrete base, they can be broken up from above with the use of a heavy hammer; however, where the tiles are secured to a timber sub-floor, the tiles should be prised up on each side using a heavy-duty scraper. Whichever method you use, it is important to remember that ceramic tiles are glazed, and smashing them can produce shards of glazing: eye protection must therefore be worn at all times.

When the tiles have been removed, check over the sub-floor surface for signs of dampness before re-laying the floor. Damage to the sub-floor should always be kept to a minimum, though it can be covered with this type of flooring without the risk of damage from lumps and bumps, unlike with vinyl tiles.

Wood-strip flooring and wooden floorboards are unlikely to provide the regular stability that is required for a ceramic-tiled floor. Such flooring surfaces should either be covered by a suitable flooring sheet such as plywood, or removed altogether and replaced with the latter.

WOOD-STRIP FLOORING

Older-style wood-strip flooring consisted of small hardwood blocks (parquet) laid onto a concrete or timber sub-floor, or softwood strips (floorboards) secured to timber joists. In the majority of cases, as with vinyl tiles, existing wood-strip flooring need not necessarily be removed before the new floor covering is laid. Make sure that

Scrub off oil and grease marks.

Floor Preparation

loose and damaged strips are secured and repaired, and it should then provide the ideal base for any other type of flooring. If, however, the wood-strip flooring is very old and uneven, perhaps as a result of damage it has suffered in the past through dampness or insect infestation, problems now resolved, then it must be removed, and how this is done will be dictated by the way in which the flooring is secured.

A wood-strip floor laid over a concrete base should be removed very carefully, checking for damage in the damp-proof membrane (this prevents damp from rising though the floor). A floorboard floor can be removed more easily, and in the right circumstances, underfloor insulation installed before the new floor covering is laid.

CLEANING

Removing the existing floor covering and exposing the existing sub-floor may expose unexpected problems. Damage caused by dampness, insect infestation and/or general disrepair constitutes a structural problem and should be dealt with by a professional; holes and cracks should be easy to deal with yourself, using proprietary brands of filler suitable for this purpose. Grease, oil stains and in some cases old paint can also be removed

Steel floor-joist system.

with proprietary chemical cleaning materials. Finally, clean away all loose materials, including dust and dirt, with a vacuum cleaner to ensure the surface will allow optimum adhesion and will not damage the new floor covering.

LEVELLING

When the previous floor covering has been completely removed, as well as inspecting the sub-floor for damage you can also check levels. Of course, some

THE STEEL JOIST SYSTEM

Steel joists can provide a versatile and cost-effective alternative to traditional timber floor joists. The lightweight galvanized C-section joists offer greater spanning capabilities than equivalent-depth timber joists, giving greater design and layout options. Unlike timber joists, steel joists are impervious to insect infestation and will not warp, rot or shrink.

The joists are compatible with traditional building methods and are supplied cut to length to speed up build times. Joist hangers are provided as a simple and effective way of connecting the joists to brick and block work.

Use a brush on stubborn stains.

floor coverings, such as ceramic tile, marble and slate, will be laid to their own levels, but others, including carpet and vinyl sheet, will follow the shape of the existing sub-floor. Where levels are a problem and the floor is uneven, a floor-levelling compound, cement-based and often very quick-drying, can be used (being careful to follow the manufacturer's instructions) to level out the low spots in the problem areas.

To find these spots, place a straight-edge in various locations over the floor surface, and circle the low areas with chalk or pencil lines. Once identified, add the levelling compound in thin layers, feathering the edges finely to finish off each layer. Try not to level off really low areas in one go. Allow each application to dry before adding further layers, continuing until the low spot is removed; then after the compound has set, any high points and bumps can be scraped off using a sharp metal scraper.

MEASURING UP

Measuring the floor area must be done accurately. If you are employing a flooring contractor to supply and fit the floor

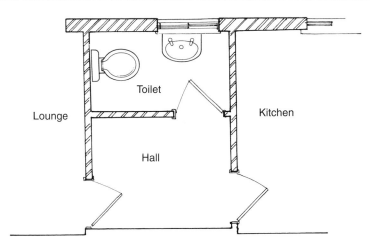

covering, he will visit the site and take the appropriate measurements, and he will then be responsible for supplying the correct quantity of materials and any fixings that may be required. If, however, you are employing a flooring contractor on a labour-only basis, it will be your responsibility to supply the correct quantity of materials plus any fixings. To reduce the risk of miscalculating the various amounts, arrange for the contractor to visit the site and supply an accurate list of materials: this may help to reduce wastage, which will inevitably save money.

Different rooms may require different surfaces.

Hire a door-trimming saw to accommodate new flooring.

Floor Preparation

The third option is to do it yourself, which may well appeal as a potential money saver – although things may not always turn out as favourably as you might imagine. It is important to purchase quantities of materials accurately, use the correct tools for the job, and recognize the need for small things to finish the job properly. Moreover, underestimating or over-ordering can be avoided, providing simple instructions are followed and care is taken in the measuring-up process.

When the area to be covered has been identified, the first important step is to find out whether the floor covering is available in metric or imperial. With this information you can add your measurements to a sheet of graph paper, working to as large a scale as the graph paper will allow, and clearly show the perimeter walls and any doors, units, fireplace and alcoves. When the floor plan is completed, and when you know the material sizes available, add these dimensions to the floor plan. Carpets and other sheet materials, including linoleum, are available in roll widths, which means that in larger rooms, one or more joins will be required. Where the carpet or

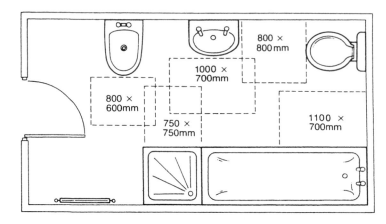

sheet material has a distinctive pattern, the location of the join may be all-important to continue the pattern effectively; so know the material and check these points before ordering. Where a join is required, make sure it falls in an area where less 'traffic' is expected. And if you are at all unsure about the measuring-up process, take a copy of your floor plan to the retailer, or ask him to call in and measure the floor for you: he can then advise you regarding joins and quantities.

Allow for working areas around units.

Installing services through steel joists.

Calculating the quantity of floor tiles, whether hard or soft, required to cover the area will depend upon the individual size of each tile. By adding the tiles individually to the floor plan a calculation can be made, unless you are using extremely small tiles. First mark a starting-point on the plan: this will show where you will start laying out the tiles, perhaps the centre point in the room. From this diagram not only can you determine the quantity of tiles required, but also where the cut tiles will be, and how these can be reduced. Wastage can be expensive, so reducing the number of cut tiles to a minimum must be built into the equation. Where tiles are bought in packs you will be able to calculate the number of packs required, and then, from the laying instructions, you can calculate how much fixing material and grout will be needed.

Where the floor covering is wooden strip flooring you must first calculate the overall floor area. To do this, multiply the widest point of the room by the longest point, then add on any alcoves, or take out areas such as fireplaces and where there are fixed units. You can then apply that calculation to the measurement the materials can be purchased in, always allowing enough extra to cover wastage.

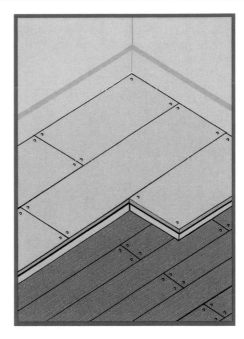

Reduce noise problems with acoustic flooring.

For expensive flooring materials, including marble and slate, cutting is best kept to an absolute minimum; so give your retailer a copy of the floor plan, and he can then calculate an accurate materials list, and arrange for any cuts to be made.

4 UNDERFLOOR HEATING

Underfloor heating is fast becoming the accepted form of heating for both domestic and commercial buildings, and is reputedly the simplest way to heat any room, be it large or small, evenly, efficiently and comfortably. Over the past decade, and following in the footsteps of European designers and specifiers, the demand for underfloor heating has grown significantly, particularly in the colder northern countries where energy efficiency is vital. This is thanks partly to advances in modern technology, and partly to the improvements in insulation of the modern home. This form of heating has proved to be energy efficient, totally safe, silent, and maintenance free, and above all it creates an enviable situation where homeowners enjoy both greater comfort and lower fuel bills.

Warm air rises creating comfort level.

When you look at the last two points individually, it is clear why demand is also growing from within the building construction industry. The first point,

Underfloor heating before the floor screed is laid.

30

that of greater comfort, has been widely tested, and it is clear that this heating system is currently the best that modern science and technology can devise. And the second point, lower fuel bills, is a result of energy efficiency that has been built into the structure of the building; the results of a survey show a clear saving when underfloor heating is compared with other methods of heating. Underfloor heating is not new, but now, with these clear advances in research, technology and home insulation, it is fast becoming the heating system of the future.

Heating plays a very important role in our daily lives because we spend more and more time indoors. For this reason the indoor climate must be right, even though it is created artificially; and in order for it to work properly, it must be supported by adequate and suitable ventilation in and around the living areas.

Designing an underfloor heating system will involve several factors, including wall construction, ceiling heights, glazing, insulation and, of course, the proposed floor covering. The system can be installed at ground-floor level, and also at first-floor level, where all rooms, and in particular the tiled floors of kitchens and bathrooms, will benefit greatly from this heat source. During the selection process you will find that the vast majority of flooring materials have been proven to react kindly to underfloor heating, though it may be reassuring just to see how the manufacturer of the flooring material you intend to use views what effect this heating method has.

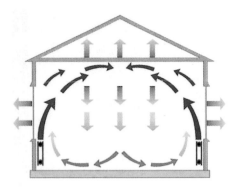

The result of underfloor heating.

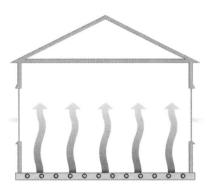

Radiators – Uneven and inefficient heat distribution

Underfloor heating – Near perfect for comfort and economy

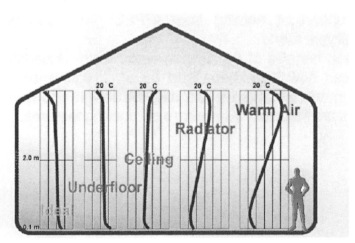

Temperature distribution of heating systems.

Underfloor Heating

Of course, the main principle of underfloor heating is not new, and is based on the simple fact that 'warm air rises'. In a central heating system designed principally around radiators, the heat starts to rise some way from the floor, creating a ceiling temperature significantly higher than the floor temperature; by comparison, underfloor heating has clear advantages. Another significant point is that underfloor heating is hidden neatly away, so you can have complete freedom of interior design, and furniture can be placed where it looks and functions best. It ensures there are no cold corners or cold floors, so that your feet are a few degrees warmer than your head, as is required for ideal comfort. The entire floor is heated, and warmth is radiated evenly and gently, with the result that there are no draughts or cold spots. A further significant point is that there are very few restrictions on floor coverings: thus you can have warm tiled floors in kitchens and bathrooms, and warm wooden and carpeted floors, all affecting the whole ambience of the room and helping to create a very pleasant comfort level.

There is also a significant saving on space, since with the underfloor heating system, the floor itself acts as the radiator, and this of course maximizes both wall space and interior design options. Thus the positioning of furniture will be

Installing underfloor heating pipes.

forever simpler, and the task of decorating greatly reduced in hardship, with no more radiators to paint.

The floor surface temperature used in underfloor heating applications is generally between 25°C and 27°C. This is lower than the body temperature and, unlike wall-hung radiators, eliminates the risk of burns to children and the elderly. The heat transfer with this type of system is mainly radiant, and therefore does not rely on air movement; this minimizes the circulation of airborne dust and reduces the likelihood of allergic respiratory reactions.

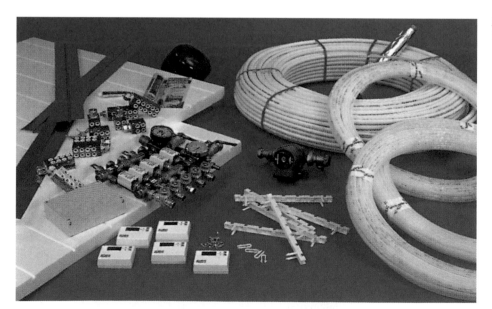

A complete underfloor heating kit.

There are currently two main forms of underfloor heating: the first is electrical, and the second is a hot water system. Both can be used with most types of floor finish or covering, and of course are completely tucked away out of sight. The electrical system is a series of thin-profile, double-insulated cables attached to an open-weave mat. The system complies with all the current electrical safety requirements, even allowing for use in wet areas such as bathrooms and kitchens. The cables are positioned at specific 'centres' ensuring an even heat distribution, and the matting silently warms the surface of the floor to an even temperature. This type of heating is easy to install on any solid-based and level floor, prior to laying the floor covering.

The 'warm' water-based system is formulated from a continuous run of polyethylene-type tubing, and there are several methods of installation, though the heating system must be positioned above the layer of floor insulation. At

Underfloor heating offers more space for furniture.

first-floor level, and perhaps in floating floors, the pipes are laid on aluminium diffusion plates in order to prevent downward heat transmission. These plates will also help to disseminate the heat. The heating pipes are designed to be resistant to any build-up of lime scale,

Underfloor heating suits most floor coverings.

33

Underfloor Heating

and to the normal levels of chlorine found in the domestic water system.

When the pipes and plates are in place, the floor covering can then be laid. The maintenance of underfloor systems is likely to be minimal because the heating element will not corrode or scale.

The benefits of this type of heating system are clear, and its installation in new buildings is increasing as people become more aware of its advantages. In most of the countries of mainland Europe, and in particular where insulation requirements are higher than in the UK, underfloor heating has already become the preferred form of domestic central heating.

Installing underfloor heating in a suspended timber floor.

5 HEALTHY FLOORING

When we select a floor covering we will, of course, consider many factors, including colour, style, life expectancy and durability – but there is one significant point of consideration frequently overlooked, and that is the impact that our choice will have on our family's health. Of course, in the vast majority of cases it will have no effect whatsoever; but with the number of allergic asthma sufferers growing year by year, it is important to be aware of it. For this very reason The Healthy Flooring Network was founded in the year 2000 by a group of individuals concerned about health, asthma and allergy. Their aims are to raise awareness of the links between fitted carpets, PVC flooring and health, and to encourage and promote alternatives.

High on the list of risks to health is the widespread use of chemicals, resins and synthetics in the production of floor coverings. Admittedly the use of these products has dramatically increased our choices in colour, and also the durability of the product; but there is a significant 'down side' to these advantages – namely that the most popular product and bene-

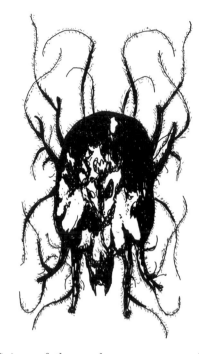

Dust mite.

ficiary of these advances, carpets, has proved to be a haven for pests and allergens.

Subtle, symmetrical and healthy.

Healthy Flooring

As much as the number of homes with wall-to-wall carpets, for so long the epitome of luxury, has increased throughout the country, so also has the number of asthma sufferers, in particular, grown significantly; recent records show that an estimated three million adults and children are now required to carry some form of medication or inhaler for daily use. Of course, the exact cause of this increase is a matter of conjecture; but today's well insulated, centrally heated and fully carpeted home has been singled out as a prime suspect.

YOUNG CHILDREN

Modern carpets and carpet fibres are manufactured and treated with chemicals to improve durability, stain resistance, moth resistance and anti-static, and their use is increasing all the time. However, these chemicals can release toxic fumes into the air over a long period of time, producing an invisible hazard that puts children, and very small children in particular, at high risk: their proximity to the surface area, plus their small size and immaturity, makes them highly susceptible to these pollutants inhaled in a concentrated form. Add to this the fact that carpeted areas also act as a sponge for cat allergens, cigarette smoke, dust mites and mould, it is no wonder that over three times the number of children suffer from breathing problems when compared to adults.

A mirror image.

DUST MITES

Dust mites are tiny, virtually invisible individuals that live primarily on the dead skin cells regularly shed from humans and pets, and they can be found in large quantities in carpeting and bedding. Just like their human benefactors, dust mites like nothing better than to live in a warm home with fitted wall-to-wall carpets, soft mattresses and warm, dry pillows. For most people the dust mite is completely harmless: it has adapted to live comfortably alongside us, and fortunately it doesn't bite. But for asthma and allergy sufferers, the inhalation of mite allergens from droppings can create a serious allergic reaction.

The life cycle of a dust mite is approximately three months, but because they have small suckers on their legs, no amount of cleaning or vacuuming will completely remove them from carpets or bedding. Nevertheless, careful and diligent control is effective, and reduces the exposure to allergen sufferers in the home.

The best form of control must be effectively to reduce their environment, and to increase the cleaning programme. This can be achieved very successfully by limiting the use of wall-to-wall carpets, and by putting down a floor surface that can be cleaned easily, with rugs or mats that can also be removed and cleaned.

Pet allergens can also be a problem.

Clean lines with eye-catching distinction.

ADHESIVES AND SEALANTS

Adhesives and sealants used when installing carpets may also pose a risk, because they emit hazardous chemicals. However, there are systems where the carpet is simply tacked to the floor, rather than stuck. Note, too, that many adhesives and finishes contain volatile organic compounds (VOCs); however, low VOC and non-VOC products are widely available. Also, a number of smooth floorings require adhesives or sealants for installation, and some of these contain polyurethane and PVC: these should be avoided.

PVC

PVC flooring contains a number of additives in large quantities, some of which are toxic. In particular the softeners known as 'phthalates' can leak out of PVC floors when they are washed, or they can be emitted into the air and attach to dust. Other hazardous additives used in PVC floors are chlorinated 'paraffins' and 'tributyl tin', chemicals that are listed internationally for priority elimination. Furthermore, there is some evidence that the 'phthalates' in PVC flooring are linked to the development of asthma, so although PVC is undoubtedly the cheapest smooth flooring, it should not be recommended as a suitable substitute for fitted carpets, particularly if there is concern about asthma or other allergies.

ASTHMA

Asthma is a chronic inflammatory disorder of the lungs and airways, which affects the ability to breathe and causes recurrent episodes of coughing, wheezing and tightness of the chest. This inflammation makes the airways very sensitive to airborne allergens from carpets, bedding, furnishings, animals, pollen, occupational irritants, pollutants and to viral infections.

DUST MITES

Dust mites are usually found at their highest concentration in beds and bedding, but by area, the greatest contamination is found in carpets. The levels found in soft furnishings almost match the levels found in beds, with clothing and soft toys also showing very high numbers of mites. The level of mites found in homes with fitted carpets is dramatically higher than homes with smooth floors, with the concentration of mites increasing with the age of the carpet.

PET ALLERGENS

The distribution of pet allergens common to cats and dogs is greater in a home with pets than one without, and more common in living rooms than in bedrooms. These allergens can also be introduced by visiting pet owners. Cat and dog allergens can be found in greater quantities in soft furnishings and upholstery, and can also be carried on clothing. Even when a pet is removed from the home environment the allergens can linger for years, having an effect when sufferers move to a new home that has previously contained a cat or a dog. Removal of all carpets will help to reduce the contamination.

Oyster schist.

Over the past three decades asthma in the United Kingdom has become increasingly prevalent. More than 3.4 million children and adults carry an inhaler with them on a daily basis: one in seven schoolchildren, and one in twenty-five adults suffer from the disease. There is much discussion about the initial cause of asthma, but it is widely accepted that asthma attacks are brought on by many types of indoor and outdoor air pollution.

Increases in asthma over the last thirty years have been in perennial, or recurrent asthma. The strongest risk factor that has been identified is sensitization to indoor allergens.

Dr T. Platt-Mills, MD,
University of Virginia

Asthma can be 'managed' by medication, to alleviate the symptoms. However, it is important to focus on identifying and reducing the allergens causing the sensitization, to prevent them from developing in the first place. For this reason, and to raise awareness and offer alternatives, The Healthy Flooring Network has produced two important lists of guidelines: the first is called *What Can Be Done At Home*, and is a guide to help reduce allergens in your home; the second, called *Alternative Flooring*, suggests suitable alternatives. These may help both to relieve allergy sufferers of their symptoms, and substantially reduce the risk of infants becoming sensitized in the first place.

Cool elegance.

Healthy Flooring

WHAT WE CAN DO AT HOME

Consider alternatives – especially if you have young children or are pregnant, or anyone in your family has asthma or allergies. Prioritize the bedroom and the living room, where people spend most of their time. Plan to take out the carpets, and as an additional measure try to keep other soft furnishings to a minimum.

If you are moving to a new home or considering refurbishing (especially if the room concerned is a nursery), choose smooth, non-PVC flooring.

Consider smooth flooring at entrances where dust and dirt can be tracked in from outside, and in 'wet' areas such as the kitchen and bathroom.

Wipe your feet. A good doormat will eliminate some of the outside dust from being tracked inside. Consider removing your shoes before you enter the house.

If you have pets, consider keeping them outside or confined to just one room. Much as we love them, they can exacerbate asthma by shedding asthma-triggering 'dander'. Frequent vacuuming can help remove 'pet' allergens.

Dispose of wet carpet. Carpet that has been wet for over a day is likely to have mould or mildew contamination that is very difficult to control. Rather than risk breeding these allergens or exposing people to toxic treatments, most experts recommend removing the wet carpet.

Avoid adhesives if possible. You can specify tack-less strips at room perimeter. Specify low-VOC seam sealant. If adhesive *is* needed, use only solvent-free, low VOC products.

If you can't remove the carpet, try and clean it often and thoroughly using a good quality, high efficiency particulate air (HEPA) vacuum – although it won't remove dust mites, it will effectively tackle animal allergens and other dust particles. Traditional vacuum cleaners may just recirculate the smaller particles back into the atmosphere.

Schedule any necessary carpet installation to allow as much time as possible for ventilation before the space is occupied again. Try to ensure the carpet has a dense, tight weave that prevents the build-up of so much dust, and is made of natural materials.

Clean old carpet before removal, as it will contain dust and dirt that can be released back into the building when it is pulled up. After removal, clean the space underneath as dust and contaminants may have been trapped there.

Floor and furniture in harmony.

ALTERNATIVE FLOORING

Natural Cork

Natural cork is taken from the bark of cork oaks, grown in the Mediterranean region as part of an ancient sustainable ecosystem. The bark is stripped from the trees every nine years, and then allowed to regrow. Cork provides a warm, rich-looking and durable flooring, and is available in many designs and colours, in tile and roll, with untreated or sealed surfaces (though avoid cork sealed with PVC). It has excellent insulation and noise-reduction qualities, making it ideal for any room in the house; also it is extremely durable, as it can be renovated. Cork underlay is supplied in rolls and sheets for use as acoustic insulation of hardwood, linoleum and laminated flooring.

Wood Flooring

Wood provides an extremely durable, hard-wearing flooring surface, and reclaimed wood or salvaged wood floors are increasingly available. If, however, you are thinking of using wood as a flooring, there are a few important questions to bear in mind.

Wood can be treated to protect it against attack from insects, fungi or mould, so be sure to check if the wood you intend to use has been treated with any substance. Treatments containing low-toxicity boric acid as a preservative are available, so be sure to ask. All the finishes and adhesives selected for installation should be solvent free or low emission.

If you are sanding down existing wooden floorboards, protect yourself from exposure to wood dust. If you have arranged for contractors to install the flooring, check that they are following proper health and safety procedures to protect both you and themselves.

Laminates

Wood laminates are made from pieces of wood glued or bonded together, and sometimes formaldehyde resins have been used to do this. These emit formaldehyde gas at room temperature, so be sure to ask for low- or zero-emitting boards.

Where excellence comes naturally.

Healthy Flooring

Natural Linoleum

Natural linoleum is very durable; it is also flexible, and acts as a good sound absorber. It is warm to the touch and available in a wide variety of colours. It is naturally anti-bacterial, anti-static, and resistant to fats and oils. Linoleum continues to get stronger over time, and has an expected life span of thirty to forty years. It is a low-maintenance product that does not require regular waxing, and is easy to clean.

Linoleum is constructed from renewable materials such as linseed oil, resin from pine trees, and wood flooring made from deciduous trees and cork, mixed together with inorganic fillers such as clay and chalk.

Bamboo Flooring

Bamboo is a relatively new product on the European market. It is very hard and strong, and can be laminated into solid boards. Bamboo shoots are harvested every four or five years, then cut and milled into long strips. Bamboo regenerates itself without the need for replanting, matures within three years, and requires little pesticide or fertilizer application. If installing bamboo, check what preservatives are used by the manufacturer; low-toxicity boric acid is best.

Jute Rugs

Jute is a very flexible vegetable fibre. It is static free so won't attract dust, and is hard wearing, sound absorbent and a good insulator; these qualities make it ideal for use on stairwells or as a rug. Tight-weave rugs are available in a wide variety of designs and patterns.

Natural Grass Rugs

Made of sisal, coir or seagrass, grass rugs have excellent noise-absorbent, thermal and anti-static qualities. Seagrass is considered to be the strongest of the grass plants. Sisal fibre comes from the henequen plant, native to Mexico; no pesticides or chemical fertilizers are used in sisal production, and although herbicides are occasionally used, even this impact may be eliminated since most weeding is done by hand. Some manufacturers treat the leaves with borax, and sisal fibres are dyed to the required fashion colours. The fibres are spun into thick yarns that contain irregularities typical of natural fabrics. Tight-weave rugs are preferable.

Sealed cork floor tiles are a healthy alternative.

6 ROOM BY ROOM

For most of us the ultimate aim is to create a sense of space and ostentation within the context of our existing surroundings, and the right choice of flooring and floor covering is the best way we can start to achieve this. Whether we are maintaining a sense of time and period in an older property, or simply making a statement of our beliefs and origins in modern surroundings, the floor area is the starting point, the palette for all our expressions. In a more global sense, mankind has always, the world over, and over the centuries, used flooring and furnishings to reflect where he lives, the prevailing climate and his social status. Thus in early Roman times, floors throughout southern European and Mediterranean countries were constructed from mosaic and marble, using materials found locally; these were found to be the perfect natural products for flooring purposes, and have, for centuries, proved to be the ideal surface: cool and classical, rich in colour, stylish in design, and hugely practical in the hot and dusty climate.

Oyster schist.

Make your decision, then sleep on it.

43

Room by Room

By direct comparison, an English country cottage often had a not dissimilar floor constructed from stone flags — like marble, stone would also have been a readily available totally natural product, and one which, from the practical aspect of being hygienic and low maintenance, ideally suited a country dwelling. By contrast, in the towns and cities a floor would more likely be constructed from timbers extracted from local forests and laid as floorboards. The raw, planed and washed boards provided a warm and acceptable surface available in a variety of colours or grains, and would be constructed from a variety of timbers, both hardwood and softwood, each with its own individual character.

Other floor coverings, such as carpets, rugs and matting, also date back many centuries: carpets woven from materials including wool and rags, animal skin rugs and rush matting, all have their place in the history of floor coverings. It was only in the late eighteenth century with the invention of mechanical looms that man-made floor coverings became more widely available, and the selection process began to gather pace. Where previously carpets and rugs were of oriental origin and a sign of affluence, during this period the appearance of 'home-grown'

Chirvan Panel in red.

carpets and rugs began to change the whole character of floor coverings in British homes. The change was slow at first, but it soon gathered pace, and from being a luxury, the carpet increasingly became an acceptable home furnishing, both as a draught reducer and for its insulating qualities.

A floor surface at any level can be laid either as a group of individual selections designed around a particular theme, or as a single floor covering with separate additions, such as rugs or throws, that help to establish the overall ambience. On the ground floor for example, a highly polished hardwood floor can be installed throughout, with perhaps a scattering of rugs selected to create the appropriate feeling for each area of the living space. Alternatively the kitchen area could be stone, hard-wearing and workable, almost bringing the outdoors into the house. By contrast, the flooring for the dining area, a warmer, more relaxing room in character, could perhaps be a hardwood, covered with an Eastern-style rug; and the lounge, where furnishings should be the epitome of relaxation and comfort, could be carpeted luxuriously, offering a single note of ostentation. With such a delightful blank canvas the home-owner can weave his own artistic spell on each and every room, pursuing all available possibilities to create a home of choice.

(*opposite*) A personal note.

Turkish splendour.

KITCHEN FLOORING

The choice of materials available today for kitchen flooring is quite staggering – flagstones, wooden strips, ceramic tiles, marble, vinyl sheets and carpets figure highly in the range of possibilities – but the key to selection lies in how well suited your choice is to the area where it is to be used. The materials for a kitchen floor should be easy to clean, durable and attractive to look at; a great deal of time is spent in and around the kitchen, so appearance – and possibly over a long period – is of prime importance. Another consideration is that, because the kitchen is the second wettest room in the house (after the bathroom), the floor must be water resistant and non slip, so when porous materials such as wood are used, they must be sealed according to the manufacturer's instructions.

Much more suitable are hard-wearing materials such as stone, quarry tiles and ceramic tiles that, when sealed properly, will fulfil nearly all the criteria required and provide an attractive end product. Water-absorbent materials such as carpets are not best used in this environment, and could be dangerous.

Magny limestone with Rosso Assiago insets.

Stone

Stone is a natural flooring material, it is extremely hard wearing, and although expensive, it requires little aftercare and should last a lifetime. After a stone floor is laid, it should be sealed with a suitable water-based sealant – though be sure to check what effect the sealant has on the natural floor colour before you use it.

Softwood can be so appealing.

Old English styling.

Quarry Tiles

Quarry tiles are the traditional flooring in kitchens, and are ideal for this purpose. They are made from high silica alumina clay, then fired for hardness. A quarry-tile floor can be laid directly onto the existing floor screed, though be sure to check what effect the additional thickness will have on the operation of doors and other fixtures. When laid, the quarry tiles will be grouted using a cement-based grout. Do not leave excess grout on the tiles to dry out, as it may result in an unwanted stain. Quarry tiles are easy to clean, and are water resistant when sealed properly.

Ceramic Floor Tiles

Slimmer than either stone or quarry tiles, these tiles are increasingly popular; available in a wide range of sizes, colours and patterns, they are hard wearing and have a glazed finish. And, of course, with so much walking about done in the work area of the kitchen, a non-slip surface is vital. One drawback with using ceramic tiles is that wear and tear and damage do not improve the floor, and, being less dense than the other hard floor coverings, the surface of the tiles can easily be chipped or cracked. When a tile is cracked it should be removed and a replacement fitted in order to retain the overall effect.

Vinyl Flooring

Vinyl is a very popular and easy-to-lay floor covering. It is available in both sheet and tile form, in a wide variety of colours and patterns, and is also available with a cushioned effect. When compared with stone and ceramic tiles, a vinyl floor will be a lot cheaper to install; it will also be easier on the feet than the harder alternatives – though of course it will not last in the same way.

If you are not sure whether to use vinyl tiles or sheet vinyl, then consider the wear and tear the floor will have to endure: if some areas will be used more than others, then tiles may be the best

The warmth of softwood flooring.

bet. Vinyl does wear with the traffic of many feet, so if sheet vinyl were used, the whole floor would need to be replaced, whereas with tiles only the worn ones would need changing. With this in mind, be sure to buy a few extra tiles just in case the colour and style you choose becomes a discontinued line.

Slate working area.

48

Installing a Stone or Tile Floor

Stone, quarry tiles and ceramic tiles and vinyl are all ideal kitchen floor coverings, easy to clean and maintain. Installation, however, is a rather different matter. A new stone floor will require a great deal of preparation, including a careful selection of materials and possible excavation works: this is definitely a job for the professionals. Both quarry and ceramic tiles, on the other hand, can be laid by the competent do-it-yourself enthusiast, though a great deal of planning is required to achieve the best results.

Vinyl flooring and vinyl tiles are much simpler floor coverings, and are both easy to cut – a sharp knife or a pair of scissors should suffice – and easy to lay; but just remember that when laying tiles, errors can be put right by replacing tiles, but this is not so easy when laying sheet vinyl flooring.

Carpet Tiles

The kitchen floor, like the bathroom, is not the best environment for water-absorbent materials such as carpet, because the latter will be difficult to keep hygienically clean and dry, and could endanger health. Carpet tiles, on the other hand, are available for use in this special environment – although when using tiles, it is important that they are secured to the surface using a proprietary double-sided tape or glue to ensure stability and safety. Nevertheless, when the tiles are stained or soiled they can be easily replaced. Like vinyl tiles and sheet vinyl floor coverings, carpet tiles are easy to install by the competent amateur.

Tiling to match the units.

Cork floor tiles at home in the kitchen.

Insets do the trick.

BATHROOM FLOORING

The bathroom is the wettest room in the house, so the floor covering you use must be suitable for the purpose. You may choose carpet because it can give a feeling of luxury and is warm to walk on, and soft under bare feet. Loose-lay bathroom carpet tiles may also be a good idea because they can be rotated to reduce wear; but whatever you choose, it should be quick drying and easy to keep clean. The synthetic materials from which bathroom carpets are made are specially designed for this purpose; even around the toilet area, which can be unhygienic, the carpet or carpet tiles should be easy to remove and clean when necessary. Unlike other rooms in the house, when the flooring is laid in a bathroom it is advisable to leave it unsecured around the edges for easy removal.

Vinyl flooring is another warm alternative ideal for the bathroom. It is easy to lay and to keep clean, and is available in a wide range of colours. Cushioned vinyl is also very good, being warmer than the non-cushioned vinyl; it will also last for many years. If you want to create various designs, or just feel that tiles are an easier option to lay, then vinyl tiles are a comparatively inexpensive floor covering and look extremely effective.

Another warm and quiet floor covering is the cork tile. These tiles are very easy to lay, but they should be the type with the sealed finish.

Wooden strip flooring is becoming very popular in various rooms around the house, including bathrooms. The timber must be sealed to prevent water penetration, and must be of a type suitable for this wet and steamy environment.

Of the harder and colder flooring tiles, ceramic floor tiles will be the most popular; however, they are likely to be the most expensive covering, and must be suitable as a flooring material, with a non-slip finish. The range of colours, shapes and styles available is very extensive, but laying them directly onto a

wooden floor should only be done after having taken professional advice. Modern houses generally have upgraded chipboard sheets in the bathroom, which have been treated before being installed, and securing ceramic tiles on these should be acceptable if the manufacturers agree; but if the floor is of floorboards, it could have an uneven finish, in which case a sheet covering may be needed before the tiles are laid. And, of course, ceramic tiles are cold to walk on and will attract some condensation when the bathroom is in use. Smaller carpets laid on the tiles will create the right balance, but they should also have a non-slip backing.

Thoroughly modern.

(opposite) Hand-finished terracotta floor.

(left) Another flooring dimension.

Room by Room

BEDROOM FLOORING

The best way to start the day is to wake up in comfortable and pleasant surroundings. So although you may spend comparatively little time in your bedroom, it is worth making sure that the style is a true reflection of your taste and personality, and that it is decorated and furnished to provide a relaxing atmosphere.

But a bedroom is not just a room in which we sleep: there are countless other activities to consider, with watching television, listening to music and reading all high on the list. Not forgetting, of course, that it may also be a room for intimacy and mood creation, or an escape from the everyday grind: but the one thing a bedroom isn't, is insignificant. For this reason the bedroom receives more attention from house designers than any other area of the house.

Tufted carpets made from pure New Zealand wool.

(opposite) Bedroom luxury.

A room for Goldilocks?

Room by Room

Designers will reassure their customers that space is not at a premium, offering up-to-date solutions to relaxation and comfort. They also know that getting this area well laid out and balanced is extremely important – and they are not alone.

Flooring manufacturers now recognize that the design possibilities are endless, and offer a whole range of products ideal for designer bedrooms, products that maximize space and storage and occupy a high priority in the modern home. Furthermore, with the growing popularity of underfloor heating in newly built homes, materials that were previously turned down because of their 'cold' effect can now be given their chance. Of course, no one wants to get out of bed onto cold marble tiles or a plain wooden floor, even with strategically placed rugs; but with times changing, these need no longer be completely ruled out. Thus instead of wood or hard tiles, linoleum and cushioned vinyl flooring can be used in a child's bedroom, being durable and easy to clean – although for luxury and comfort, thick, plush pile carpet is still the clear favourite for this 'haven': warm and soft underfoot, its texture will always be ideal for intimacy and privacy, unlike the echoey resonance of wooden or hard tiled flooring.

All in all it is fair to say that the bedroom of the modern home is no longer just a place to sleep. It needs to be multifunctional, with careful planning given to a multitude of leisure pursuits and activities.

Luxury at all levels.

LOUNGE AND RECEPTION ROOMS

As families spend more and more time in their homes and in particular their lounge/living areas, so the selection of flooring materials for these areas must be given extra careful consideration. The reasons for this are twofold. Firstly, the lack of available space, plus the creative concepts used in modern house design, often lead to the living areas being linked together: thus lounge/dining room and kitchen/dining room can be seen frequently on floor plans, and inevitably this limits the possibilities of furnishing them individually – although it does not remove them altogether. Areas can be easily and clearly defined, and invisible boundaries erected, simply by varying the floor covering. And where two living areas are formed within one room, so the flooring can be selected for each area individually.

Secondly, whether physical boundaries exist or not, the floor covering selected is hugely representative of the occupants and, possibly, their status. For example, for centuries, plush and luxurious floor coverings have always been an

Veronique in Tartan Green.

accurate reflection of affluence, and very little has changed. The availability of quality products and quality imitations means that we can all live as the Romans lived.

Then, of course, there is the decorative order and cleanliness of the home, points that can easily be reflected in the choice of floor covering. That is why care must be taken, and simple, unqualified selection will not suffice. The most popular floor covering must be carpet, but laminated wood, floorboards, and stone or terracotta-tiled floors all have their followers. What is important is that with hard flooring – stone and marble, for example – the installation and finishing are carried out to a high standard. With carpets, too, both trimming and fitting may be better carried out by professionals.

Cork tiles add a warm touch.

It is also likely that the floor covering for these 'family' rooms will need to be multifunctional as well as representative of the decorative order of the home. The amount of traffic may well be fairly high, though not as busy as in, say, the hallway; but the floor covering must be durable, otherwise signs of wear and tear will quickly show. Floorboards, by contrast, provide a warm and appropriate backdrop in design, against which the furniture, rugs and furnishings can be moved around at will – unlike wall-to-wall carpets, where parameters and room divisions may be more apparent, and where the floor covering for each room will reflect that room's use.

Where carpets are used in every room, the defining difference may be the style or the colour. Rooms for relaxing in will benefit from subtle hues and warm, plush textures, unlike busy communal rooms, where durability and sturdiness will be important.

Parquet flooring – pure elegance.

So the first plan for the lounge or dining room is to check where the boundaries are, and to try to work within them. Where these family rooms are inseparable as a result of both wall and house construction, divisions by way of floor covering may be a good way of setting out the boundaries.

(opposite) A travertine floor.

Laminated flooring elegance.

Room by Room

And remember: creating beautiful and practical floors by using different materials, each to enhance the physical characteristics of a room, will set the style and ambience of your home.

HALLWAYS AND STAIRCASES

The hallway floor is significant in two very different ways. First, the hallway itself is likely to be the narrowest room in the house, and traffic will probably be centred over a single strip of ground – so the floor covering for this area should be particularly hard wearing, non slip and tough. It is also most likely to get dirty, so must be easy to clean. And secondly, putting these practical reasons to one side, it must be attractive and welcoming as it is the first room that visitors enter in your home, and it is therefore where their first impressions are formed.

Carpeting throughout.

Royal Turkey in redcurrant.

In modern homes, wall-to-wall carpets will be the norm, but they can become worn and dirty, and even bare wooden floorboards or flagstones can suffer from excessive use – so the choice of floor covering must take these points into account. Hard floors of stone and tile are durable and generally easy to keep clean, as well as creating just the right feeling to visitors. To protect the surface, strategically positioned rugs will add softness and warmth – though care must be taken to ensure they do not slip. Warmer floors such as wood, cushioned vinyl and carpet, can also create the right ambience, and they, too, will benefit from this type of protection.

In areas likely to suffer from excessive wear and tear, and where the introduction of dirt and grime can jade and discolour the surface, moveable protection is the answer: this might include rugs

Oriental Silk in Dark Zircon Green.

Oyster schist Jacuzzi.

and carpet protectors that can easily be rolled up and cleaned or relocated – although take care to ensure that any variance in floor level is easily seen. Accidents do happen – someone tripping over a rug or the carpet – so when you put down a surface protector or decoration, make sure they are distinctive from the existing floor. This will help both visitors and the elderly to recognize that there is a change of level in the floor surface.

Staircases, too, are likely to be carpeted, either fully or partially, the fabric held firmly in place with gripper rods. The carpet must be suitable for this very specialized purpose, and it should be fitted very securely and with extreme care. On a practical note, it is best to avoid joins in the stair carpet; but where this is inevitable, make sure the join is on a riser and not a tread, where small feet and shoe heels could be caught up. The installation of a stair carpet will fall easily within the remit of a qualified fitter. This is an installation of high complexity and the effect of it will have important repercussions on carpets both at the foot of the staircase and at the top.

Laminated flooring is easy to clean.

7 FLOORING MATERIALS

NATURAL STONE

Hundreds of millions of years ago, massive deposits of rock were formed as a result of the earth's geological activities, and these rocks have been classified into three groups: sedimentary, metamorphic and igneous. Sedimentary rock, as the name implies, has been formed by the compaction of sediment, from an ancient riverbed perhaps. This rock is the softest of the three types and includes limestone and sandstone; in the majority of cases it is very suitable for flooring.

Metamorphic rock is formed deep below the earth's surface and is the result of both heat and compaction; it is extremely common in mountainous regions. This type of rock includes marble and slate, harder wearing than sedimentary rock, but not as hard wearing as igneous rock.

Igneous rock – granite is a prime example – is extremely hard wearing. It is formed as a result of magma cooling and crystallizing, and can be found deep below the earth's surface on all the continents of the world.

Classical styling.

Slate – looks beautiful, lasts a lifetime.

61

More recently, and on a time scale of hundreds of years, as opposed to millions, these natural rocks or stones have been and are still being quarried for domestic use. Huge blocks of slate, marble, granite and sandstone are removed from the earth, and then chiselled or sawn into shape for structural use as walls, roofs and floors.

In Britain, regions can be easily identified by the local sedimentary rock used in the house-building process, while in the countries of Europe, more mountainous than Britain, granite and marble are most common. Originally the stone would have been available on the surface in the form of rocks and boulders; these would be gathered up and arranged to form a building probably quite similar to a cave in shape. But as working tools improved, and the quantity of surface rocks reduced, so quarrying started and the stone was shaped into the form of materials suitable to build walls and roofs and to lay floors.

Demand increased, and so the number of quarries grew to meet this demand. At first the stone would be removed from local quarries, and then used locally. But occasionally, wealthy landowners would become attracted to the colour and qualities of a particular stone, and they would arrange for it to be hauled across continents to build palaces and villas.

Beijing green slate.

More recently, and as a direct result of the improvements in the transport system and available information, there has been a dramatic increase in demand for specific stones quarried in certain areas. This is because stone can be so different between regions. When the rock was formed all those millions of years ago, local minerals infiltrated the structure and created a colouring that was individual to, and singularly identifiable with, that particular region: in fact, it is said that quarried stone can be almost as distinctive as fingerprints. And the colours can range from grey and red, through green, black, white, pink – in fact almost any colour can be found if you look hard enough.

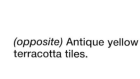

(opposite) Antique yellow terracotta tiles.

(left) Farmhouse slate steps.

LIMESTONE AND SANDSTONE FLOORS

Limestone and sandstone are the commonest form of sedimentary rock used in domestic flooring today. Formed over millions of years in river, sea and ocean beds, these sedimentary rocks consist of clay, fossils and other waste materials, and are generally available in a wide range of colours. During formation, and because sedimentary rock is not compacted under the same pressure as the other rocks, air pockets can be formed, and it is these air pockets that can give the stone its individuality. Sedimentary rocks are common in the UK, and this rock has been widely used in domestic construction for walls, roofs and floors for many centuries.

Although limestone and sandstone make an excellent building material, they need to be 'dressed' before being used – that is, each stone must be shaped and sized to its required size. After the limestone and sandstone rocks are quarried, they are then sawn into slabs of the size required for flooring. The surface is

St Arbois aged limestone.

Chipped edge fossil sandstone.

64

then polished to give it a relatively smooth finish, while emphasizing the varying layers, and also to bring out all the colours. A smoother finish can be achieved by sanding the surface, though this does eliminate some of the contours characteristic with this type of stone, and is often found to be impractical for internal floors.

The limestone and sandstone texture is porous, and will need to be sealed when used as an internal floor covering. Sealers are available, though care must be taken to ensure that the sealer used enhances the natural colours of the stone.

Another significant factor to be considered when selecting limestone or sandstone for flooring is wear and tear. As explained earlier, sedimentary rock is less dense and less compact than, for example, marble, so positioning is

important. When you have an area where excessive wear and tear is likely to affect the evenness of the floor, then measures should be taken to reduce this: strategically placed rugs may be the answer. But there are areas – just inside entrance doors may be one – where unevenness can quickly occur, and even well-placed protectors may not be able to hold back damage, so awareness of this point is important. From time to time when wear is excessive, these areas can be removed and replaced, although matching the floor colours may be difficult. Possibly the insertion of a section of a harder-wearing stone from the outset may be an idea. Whatever you decide to do, these points must be considered when planning the longevity of the floor.

Magny limestone with Rosso Assiago insets.

Cutting and Grouting

Limestone and sandstone are both soft stones and can be cut by hand; however, cutting the stone with a diamond-tipped stone cutter is advisable, and eye protection and breathing masks must be worn at all times.

Abbey Gold sandstone.

Flooring Materials

When the limestone floor is laid, the joints will need to be grouted. This can be done using a proprietary grout, applied according to the manufacturer's instructions. Again, as with the flooring adhesive, where the floor is liable to movement or flexing you must ensure the grout is suitable for this purpose, otherwise cracking around the joints may occur. To protect the floor surface from damage, or discoloration and staining by the grout, a 'limestone impregnator' or similar protection can be applied, with a brush, and in two or three coats. When the floor is ready, the joints can be filled with grout – but take care to keep grout off the floor surface. Push the grout firmly and evenly into the joints, and then remove any excess with a damp cloth. Leave to dry before sweeping or sealing the floor.

Maintenance

Limestone is classified as a chalky, porous rock, and sealing is recommended when it is used as a flooring material. Extra care must be taken when limestone or sandstone is used in areas where there is a risk from oil and water absorption; this will include kitchens and bathrooms.

MARBLE FLOORS

Marble is formed from the process of sedimentary rocks, such as limestone, being crushed together and heated, as a result of movement around the earth's crust over many millions of years. The pressure and heat generated by this movement caused the limestone to tighten up in texture, and the calcium carbonate then crystallized to form marble. This 'metamorphosis' turned the rock from being a sedimentary rock into a metamorphic one, as the name suggests. Another effect of this crushing process was that the new rock, commonly known as marble, was very brittle, so mining has to be carried out in a very controlled way; it is totally unsuitable for the type of quarrying where explosives are used. Also, unlike other metamorphic rocks such as slate, marble does not have clearly defined seams, and therefore it does not split easily into sheets. For this

Negev limestone.

(opposite) **Magny limestone with Rosso Assiago insets.**

St Briare CE limestone.

LAYING FLOOR TILES
1) Make sure the floor is clean and free from oil and grease.
2) Always mix the adhesive according to the manufacturer's advice.
3) First apply a layer of adhesive on to the clean surface using the flat side of the trowel.
4) Then using the notched side of the trowel, add another layer of adhesive at a 45° angle to the surface. Spread only enough adhesive at one time for 10min tiling.
5) Push the tile into the adhesive, and twist slightly to ensure grip. Use a wooden block or rubber mallet to level the tiles.
6) Clean off the tiles with a damp sponge as you go along, removing excess adhesive.

GROUTING
1) Mix the grouting according to the manufacturer's recommendations.
2) Spread the grout over the joins using a rubber float, pushing the grout into the joints until they are completely filled.
3) Remove excess grout from the face of the tiles using the rubber float.
4) Remove remaining grout with a damp sponge (not wet), working across and not along the joints. Allow time to dry.
5) After 24hr, wipe over the floor with clean water and buff up with a clean cloth.

reason it is extracted from the quarry using specialized rock-cutting machinery, and the extracted rock is then cut into slabs or tiles of varying thickness and size, depending on its intended use.

Marble has grown in demand throughout the centuries because of one very significant quality: its colour. White marble is, of course, the purest, and has proved to be very popular with sculptors; however, as a direct result of the crushing process closing the texture, marble can be seen in an almost overwhelming array of patterns as well as in white. Add to this the variety of local conditions where natural compounds are introduced, usually specific to that particular area, and you will get a marble in a wonderful array of colours that are found only in that region. That is the reason why almost all marbles are named after the region in which they are quarried.

Travertine flooring.

SE travertine with marble border.

SE travertine flooring.

Flooring Materials

Marble is excellent for use in the home, and in particular for working tops and as flooring, because its close texture dramatically reduces its porosity; this means that it is especially suitable in areas where water is used a lot, such as the bathroom. However, although marble is very tough and dense, it is nonetheless susceptible to staining when it comes in contact with certain acids, so its use in the kitchen, in particular, should be limited, and it should be treated with extreme care. Where marble is installed in these areas, the surface should be properly sealed and a finish applied.

The finished floor surface can be gloss or matt, with the latter probably more appropriate for a floor; the surface can then be sealed or polished according to requirements. As with all cold stone floors, it will benefit hugely from under-floor heating.

Marble mosaic.

SE travertine with marble border.

Designers have used marble flooring as a decoration for centuries. In Italy, where a vast array of marble is quarried, examples of marble floors, statues and columns are numerous. And with so many colours to choose from, and because the surface is so hard, a variety of shapes can be cut and an array of patterns produced.

Cutting

Marble is a harder rock than limestones and sandstones, though it is still classified as 'soft' when compared to igneous rocks such as granite. A water-cooled, diamond-tipped stone cutter will be required for cutting, though this is best done by a professional. When cutting any stones it is always advisable to wear eye protection and a breathing mask at all times.

Marble border in travertine floor.

Magny limestone with Rosso Assiago insets.

Grouting

When a marble floor is laid, the joints will need to be grouted, with the joint size according to personal taste; this is recommended at about 6–10mm. This can be done using a proprietary grout, and applied according to the manufacturer's instructions. As with flooring adhesive, where the floor is liable to movement or flexing it is important to use a suitable grout, otherwise cracking around the joints may occur. To protect the floor surface from damage or discoloration and staining by the grout, a 'marble impregnator' or similar protection can be applied, with a brush, in two or three coats.

When the floor is ready, the joints can be filled with grout, pushing it in firmly and evenly, being careful to keep it off the floor surface. Remove any excess with a damp cloth. Leave to dry before sweeping or sealing the floor.

Maintenance

Marble should be treated with a recommended sealer when used as a flooring material. Non-reflective marble performs well and requires minimum maintenance, though care must be taken when it is used in the kitchen because the surface can be damaged by oil.

Traditional hand-crafted floor tiles.

SLATE

Like marble, slate is a metamorphic rock; however, it has none of marble's textural qualities, and, unlike marble, it is produced by the compression of other materials, including shale, into parallel layers. Slate is very ancient rock, and can be found in the oldest mountainous regions of the world. For centuries it has been mined and used as a building material, though the extraction methods that were used, namely blasting, damaged a lot of the rock, leaving huge mounds of waste. Today slate is mined using modern mining techniques, where the slate blocks are first extracted from the quarry using diamond-wire saws, and these blocks are then cut to size and shape with diamond-tipped saws. Because slate is a fine-grained rock, and so can be easily split into thin sheets, it is highly suitable for flooring and roofing,

and is therefore extremely useful.

There are four or five types of slate flooring generally available, but the two styles known as 'Riven' and 'Fine Rubbed' (or polished) may be considered the most common for flooring. Riven tiles are hand split along the grain of the slate to expose a naturally textured surface; with a non-slip finish, they are ideal for any location around the home. Fine Rubbed tiles have a smoother finish, although the polished effect may vary from one tile to another. The finished effect may vary, too, but the colour of the slate seldom fades when used indoors.

Slate is a close relative of limestone and marble; however, unlike them, slate is waterproof and extremely hard wearing, though it can be susceptible to scratching. Because of its waterproof qualities it is especially useful in areas of the home where water is used a lot, such as the bathroom and the kitchen.

Beijing green slate hallway.

Cutting

Slate is a natural cleft material, so take care when cutting that it doesn't split. It is a harder and less porous rock than limestones and sandstones though, like marble and limestone, it is still classified as 'soft' when compared to granite. To cut slate you will require a water-cooled, diamond-tipped cutter, and you must follow the standard safety guidelines by wearing eye protectors and a breathing mask. Large amounts of dust will be produced, so the slate will need cleaning thoroughly after cutting and before sealing.

Cutting rocks is always best undertaken by a professional, who will use a water-cooled, diamond-tipped stone cutter. As mentioned above, when cutting any stones it is always advisable to wear eye protection and a breathing mask at all times.

Beijing green slate close up.

A slate floor will transform your kitchen.

Style and sophistication.

Flooring Materials

Grouting

When the slate floor is laid, the joints are usually very thin, though they will need to be grouted in the normal way. This can be done using a proprietary grout, applied according to the manufacturer's instructions. As with flooring adhesive, at those points where the sub-floor is liable to any movement or flexing, it is important to use a suitable grout, otherwise it may crack around the joints. To protect the floor surface from damage or from discoloration and staining by the grout, two or three coats of a 'slate impregnator' or similar protection can be applied with a brush. When the floor is ready, the joints can be filled with grout, taking care to keep it off the surface of the slates. Push the grout firmly and evenly into the joints, and then remove any excess with a damp cloth. Leave to dry before sweeping or sealing the floor.

Maintenance

Slate should be treated with a recommended sealer when used as a flooring material, though take care to ensure that all dust is removed before the sealant is applied. Slate is classified as very hard-wearing, and, as a result of this, plus the fact that it has a low absorption rate when sealed, the slate floor will require little maintenance.

GRANITE

Granite has been classified by geologists as an 'igneous' rock. It is extremely hard and coarse grained, and comprises a major part of the earth's land masses. Granite was formed many millions of years ago, when magma, a molten material, cooled slowly and crystallized, deep within the earth's crust. Volcanic magma has the same qualities but, as a result of more rapid cooling, the texture is finer.

Granite is mined throughout the world, different regions producing different characteristics. It is then cut into sheets approximately 1in (13mm) thick, and one side is polished before these are dispatched to distributors.

The hardness and durability of granite, plus its ageless, natural qualities, have not been ignored by interior design-

A slate floor in the kitchen.

ers, and granite is now widely used on work surfaces and floors in modern homes. Granite floors and other work surfaces can be expected to last a lifetime, and its beautiful colouring remains constant.

CARING FOR MARBLE
- Keep the marble dust-free.
- Use a clean mop, kept specifically for the marble floor.
- Never add vinegar to the wash, as it strips the shine.
- Remove spills of wine, alcohol and citrus juices immediately, using clean water.
- Never use metal pet bowls or similar equipment where there is a possibility of rust staining the marble.
- In bathrooms use clean water to wash away soapy spills before they cause unattractive marks and stains.

As an igneous rock a granite floor is not porous, and it is both heat and scratch resistant; this makes it very difficult to damage, and gives it a significant 'ecological' edge over other, less hard-wearing rocks, and also over man-made materials with a lower life expectancy. So although granite may be expensive at the outset, the investment may be timeless.

Cutting

Granite is an extremely hard rock, and is best cut and laid professionally. However, if you decide to cut it yourself you will require a water-cooled diamond-tipped cutter, and one that is suitable for cutting granite: it is important to specify this when you order and collect the cutter. You must also follow the standard safety guidelines by wearing eye protectors and a breathing mask, because granite must be cut slowly, and large amounts of dust will be produced.

Grouting

When the granite floor is laid, the joints can vary, though they should remain within the 6–10mm guidelines, with the

grouting applied in the usual way. This can be done using a proprietary grout, and applied according to the manufacturer's instructions. As with flooring adhesive, where the sub-floor is likely to move or flex, it is important to choose a suitable grout, otherwise it may crack around the joints. The majority of gran-

Slate – the production line.

Hand split to expose natural texture.

Flooring Materials

ites are impervious to water and are also stain resistant, but check with your supplier whether you should protect the floor surface from damage or discoloration, and from staining by the grout. If the latter circumstance is possible, then enquire about an appropriate protection against staining, and before sealing. When the floor is ready, the joints can be filled with grout, though take care to keep it off the floor surface. Push the grout firmly and evenly into the joints, and then remove any excess with a damp cloth. Leave to dry before sweeping or sealing the floor.

Maintenance

Granite is a very low-maintenance floor covering, though it should be treated with a recommended sealer before use; be sure that all dust is removed before the sealant is applied. Granite is available in a glossy finish, though this can be slippery when wet. There is also a rough or etched finish available, so take care to select the right finish for each location.

SCHIST
Schist is a slate-like stone with a high quartz and mica content; it has a sparkle, unlike slate.

TERRAZZO
Terrazzo is a man-made product composed of stone chips mixed with cement, then polished to produce an alternative to marble.

TRAVERTINE
Similar in appearance to Venetian marble; it is extremely popular for its ability to cope well in areas where traffic is high, such as hallways.

REPLACING A BROKEN TILE
1) Remove the grout from around the damaged tile, taking care not to mark or damage adjacent tiles.
2) When the grout is completely removed, using a hammer and chisel, chip away from the centre of the tile outwards until the tile is removed. Always wear eye protectors when chipping at tiles.
3) Clean the area well, removing all signs of tile and adhesive.
4) Spread a thin layer of adhesive in the gap, making sure not to get any on the adjacent tiles.
5) Press the tile firmly into place, removing any excess adhesive immediately.
6) Allow the adhesive to set before finishing off with grout.

A touch of Mexico with terracotta tones.

INSTALLATION

All stone flooring, whether limestone, marble or granite, is heavy, so the sub-floor must be strong enough to carry this type of specialist floor covering. Before you start, the damp proofing, floor insulation and underfloor heating will all need to be in place and thoroughly checked. Removing any section of the floor to carry out repairs after it is laid, grouted and sealed is not recommended.

When the base floor is cleared of debris, and if the base is an existing solid floor, it should be free from grease or oil; preparations can then be made to lay the flooring. This can be on a bed of mortar, a floor screed, or using a proprietary adhesive suitable for this purpose.

When laying stone flooring on top of a timber floor, take great care to ensure the floor has all the necessary 'load-bearing' qualities. It may then be advisable to lay a continuous polythene sheet over the base timber floor area to act as a damp-proof membrane before the flooring adhesive is laid. Make sure the adhesive is suitable for floors where some movement or flexing is likely.

Depending on the location of the floor and the atmospheric drying conditions, the floor should be ready to walk on fairly quickly.

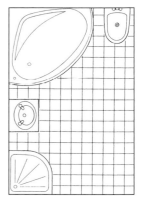

Measure for tiles to reduce wastage.

FLOOR FINISHES

Handmade: Hand-formed by local craftsmen.

Honed: Machined or hand-worked to a smooth finish.

Riven: A textured surface as a result of being split by hand.

Polished: Machine- or hand-worked to produce a polished surface.

Hand-finished: Usually made by machine and finished off by hand.

Antique: A newly quarried stone given an antique finish.

Flamed: Subjected to heat to produce a rough-textured, non-slip finish.

Antique Terracotta Blanc Rose.

Antique Jerusalem
Mosaic.

8 FLOOR TILES

TERRACOTTA TILES

The word 'terracotta' comes from the Latin, and literally speaking means 'fired earth'. Terracotta floor tiles have been produced throughout Europe for almost a thousand years, and it is this long tradition of use that has established terracotta as a leader in domestic stone floor coverings. In many areas terracotta tiles are still handmade, and it is this practice, plus the fact that a variety of local clays are used – and even the way the tiles are fired – that has for so long imbued the whole range of terracotta tiles with a vast array of colours, shapes and sizes. The tiles are unglazed and fired at a low temperature, giving them a semi-porous texture and a truly rustic appearance.

A superb maple and slate combination.

Bathroom opulence.

Terracotta tiles are more commonly machine-produced today, though some handmade tiles are still fired in small kilns throughout Europe. There is also a demand for 'used' or 'distressed' tiles, as designers strive to achieve that well-worn appearance.

Unlike the majority of floor tiles, and as a result of their unique manufacturing process, terracotta tiles are extremely porous and very susceptible to staining. When they are laid they will need to be properly sealed, using perhaps a solution of linseed oil followed by a good waxing. Adding any oil-based sealer to a porous surface will almost certainly alter the colouring of the tile, so it is always best to test the sealer on a spare tile before using it on the floor. As a direct alternative, a water-based sealant as opposed to an oil-based one may be less likely to alter the surface colour.

History has proved that terracotta flooring is a flooring for life, and it has genuinely earned the appraisal that 'a terracotta floor is just wearing in when others are wearing out'.

QUARRY TILES

Quarry tiles are almost everything terracotta tiles are not. They are a relatively modern tile, possibly only a couple of hundred years old. They are machine made for uniformity, and they are denser than terracotta, making them colder to touch. And they are fired at extremely high temperatures, which reduces their porosity dramatically and leaves the tile with a finished surface that does not require any sealant or wax.

Another well-known feature of quarry tiles (because they are mass produced) is their consistent colouring – in fact some would say too consistent, though a few manufacturers today are trying to introduce a splash of colour into the quarry tile in an attempt to reduce the uniformity. Quarry tiles are available in a range of colours allowing interior designers to plan anything from the typical 'Victorian' floor so commonly associated with quarry tiles, or a mosaic of styles and designs.

What is certain is that this extremely resilient tile with its non-slip, low-

You never had it so good!

Totally traditional.

Stylish kitchens.

porous and hard-wearing qualities is very popular, in kitchens in particular, where a hard-wearing, water-resistant floor is required.

CERAMIC TILES

Ceramic tiles are a hard tile manufactured from clay and fired at a very high temperature. They are available glazed and unglazed and in a wide choice of colours, patterns and shapes, so that with careful selection, a wide variety of effects can be created.

When you are planning a ceramic tiled floor, as with any other tile, you should consider all their features practically, both the positive and the negative ones. On the positive side, ceramic floor tiles wear extremely well, so they are ideal for use in high wear areas such as the kitchen; they are easy to keep clean; as a result of the manufacturing process they are water resistant; and they can be non slip. On the negative side, they can crack easily when something heavy is dropped on them; and, like all hard tiled floors, standing on such a hard surface for long periods may be very tiring on the legs.

INSTALLING FLOOR TILES

Before laying floor tiles, every consideration must be given to the surface upon which the tiles are going to be laid. Tiling onto a new floor screed should be relatively straightforward, though the screed must be allowed enough time to 'cure' properly. Fixing tiles to a suspended wooden floor will require more care.

Inspiration, Victorian style.

Classical Florentine styling.

Floor Tiles

Firstly the floor must have a sufficient load-bearing capacity to carry the additional weight of the tiles; and secondly, it must be rigid enough not to flex or move, as this can cause the tiles or the tile joints to crack.

When the tiles are to be laid onto an existing concrete or tiled surface, then the surface must be clean and free from grease or oil; smooth surfaces should be 'roughed up' a little to ensure adhesion. Other surfaces, including vinyl, linoleum and cork tiles, should be removed and the surface cleaned. Skirting boards, doors and architraves should be removed to allow the tiles to be laid close to walls and to achieve the best possible results.

Measuring Up

First, clear the floor area of all removable objects, and familiarize yourself with the non-removable fixtures, such as radiator pipes and kitchen units. Door positions are important, because heavy usage will eventually be the greatest test of successful floor planning.

When the room is cleared as much as is possible, and the fixtures noted, find the centre line of the room in one direction, and draw a chalk line along it. Repeat this in the opposite direction, and you should then have the centre point of the room. Do not start tiling yet, however. The next important step is to check the size of the tiles being laid, and how, by moving the lines, you can reduce the

number of cut tiles required. Be sure to include the width of grout joints in your

Trowelling on flooring adhesive.

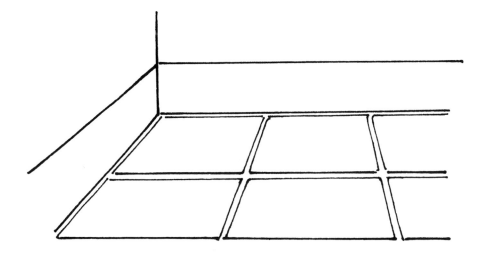

Tiling into corners.

84

Only lay a square metre of adhesive at one time.

Floor Tiles

calculations. Do not, however, if at all possible, leave a small tile strip cut along one wall. This will not be geometrically appealing, so where possible, try to leave the edges as even as you can, to provide a better look to the finished floor.

Cutting and Fixing

Following the guidelines drawn on the floor, lay the full tiles using the adhesive cement recommended for that flooring material. Spread the cement evenly over a small area, say, 1 square metre, making sure there is enough adhesive not to leave air pockets. Push the tile into the adhesive, making sure a grout joint is left around the tile edges, and also keeping adhesive off the surface of the tile. When that metre is laid, then add another metre of adhesive, and so on. Do not put down too much adhesive cement on the floor before you start laying tiles. Check the levels as you go along, keeping in mind the thickness of the tiles and checking for low or high spots in the base floor.

When the full tiles have been laid, then the cut tiles can be added. Cutting ceramic and glazed tiles can be done using either an angle grinder, where eye protection must be worn; a tile breaker,

where the tile is scored, then broken along the line; or a tile cutter, where the tile is scored, then snapped along the line. The method you use will be dictated by the type and thickness of the tile. Shapes and rough edges can be nibbled using a pair of pliers or pincers.

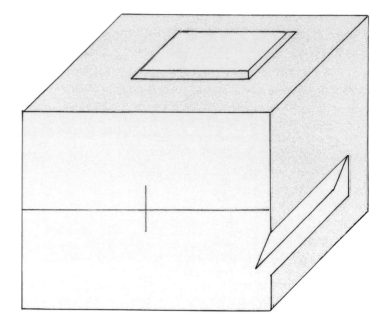

Find the centre point in the room.

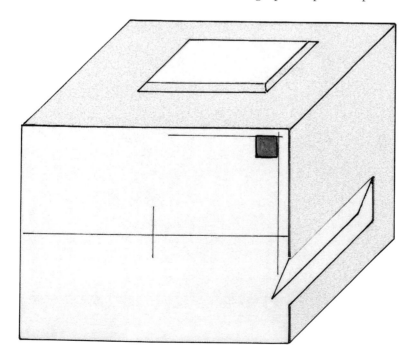

Measure out to maintain symmetry.

Grouting

When the floor is laid, the joints can be filled with a proprietary grout applied in the usual way, according to the manufacturer's instructions. As with the flooring adhesive, where the sub-floor is likely to move or flex, be sure to use a suitable grout, otherwise it may crack around the joints. The majority of floor tiles are impervious to water – terracotta tiles and others will already have been sealed before the grouting process starts – though some may stain. In these instances a stain-resistant solution may be required, so it is very important to check with your supplier whether you need to protect the floor surface from damage or discoloration and staining by the grout. If this is possible, then inquire about an appropriate protection against staining, and before sealing.

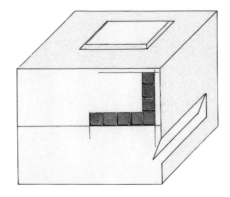

Lay a few tiles at a time.

When the floor is ready, the joints can be filled with grout, taking care to keep it off the floor surface. Push the grout firmly and evenly into the joints, and then remove any excess with a damp cloth. Leave to dry before sweeping or sealing the floor.

Venetian marble.

Sealing

Unglazed floor tiles will need to be sealed in order to protect the porous surface. The sealing will normally be carried out in two stages, the first stage after the floor is laid and before the tiles are grouted, and the second after the grouting has set. Before the first coat is laid, make sure the tiles are dry and the floor is clean; then after the grouting is completed and you are sure the grout is dry, add the second coat.

The process of sealing will differ from tile to tile, so it is important that you check with your supplier the type of sealer required and the application process.

PREVENTATIVE MAINTENANCE

The best maintenance of a hard floor is preventative. Abrasive particles of dirt and grit can scar and scratch the floor surface, reducing the overall appearance and, in the long run, the life of the floor. Sweeping the floor regularly will reduce this likelihood and is a very integral part of day-to-day maintenance. A soft broom will be ideal for smooth surfaces, and a slightly harder broom, or even a vacuum cleaner, will be better for textured surfaces.

Where dirt and grime may stick to the floor surface, damp mopping is very efficient. This should be done on a regular basis, and after the floor has been swept.

Oyster schist pool surround.

(opposite) Thar stone.

Antique stone.

Floor Tiles

It is important to wash and rinse the floor thoroughly and regularly, taking particular care to follow the guidelines applicable to the floor you have. Similarly, the soaps and detergents you use must be suitable for the floor material. Soaps, whether vegetable based or speciality soaps, are usually suitable for stone floors; detergents, however, though excellent for attacking oil and grease, must be checked for their compatibility with your floor. Detergents can also weaken any surface protection you have on the floor, wax or polish, leaving the floor unprotected and requiring further waxing or polishing.

Abrasive cleaning materials can be used on stubborn marks, but may cause damage, and should not really be used where the floor surface is polished or glossy. Bleach is very good at removing stains, but as with every tool, material or fluid you use on the floor, make sure the surface is not damaged as a result.

9 WOODEN FLOORS

There is something about the warm, timeless, natural qualities of a real wooden floor that makes it a winner in the flooring business. A wooden floor is adaptable and will generally suit almost any colour scheme, but there are other advantages, too, in that it is easy to install, it will wear extremely well, and it is not easily spoiled by stains or spills.

There are many kinds of wooden floor to choose from, all made from different woods: softwoods and hardwoods, deciduous and coniferous. Softwoods – pine, spruce and cedar for example – are grown in the evergreen, coniferous rainforests of Northern Europe, Asia and America, and the hardwoods are taken from the deciduous oak, chestnut, maple, beech and ash forests of Europe and America. Most if not all of these forests have been checked to ensure that the forestry method used is sustainable in the environment and in the survival of the species. Of course the terms 'hardwood' and 'softwood' cannot always be taken literally: not all hardwoods are hard – for instance, balsa wood is a soft hardwood – and not all softwoods are soft – yew is a hard softwood. This principle applies

Cork oak and bark.

Laminated flooring.

even within the range of individual species of wood, because there are such differences. The American oak, for example, is a faster-growing species than the English oak and therefore produces a softer, less durable wood. Also, the colours and grains within each species can vary to a dramatic extent. But this is not to the detriment of wood: in fact, it is these idiosyncrasies that makes wood so appealing and always in such demand.

Wood has been used in the construction of domestic buildings as walls, floors and roofs for centuries. Over all these years it has suffered the scourges of dry rot, insect infestation and damp; however, modern domestic building cannot survive without wood, so as a result of improved treatments and improvements in building standards, these problems have been almost eradicated.

Today, the standing of wood in the home is as strong as ever, and it is remarkable that after so much progress, little has changed in design; thus the traditional wooden floor can be the base on which other floor coverings are secured, or it can be the finished floor covering itself. Stained in any of a wide variety of colours, or polished and strewn with rugs, it is a veritable dream for the designer, a work of art creating both a

Clever planning with warm undertones.

(opposite) Brazilian cherry (jatoba).

Cork tiles in the bathroom.

Wooden Floors

healthy environment and an unmistakably cosy atmosphere.

Nevertheless, selection of the right floor covering may be less straightforward – although there are really only two main styles to choose from. The first is the traditional solid wooden floor constructed with planks of varying widths, tongued and grooved along the edges and secured to the floor joists. Commonly known as 'floorboards', they are available in both soft- and hardwoods, and the finished surface is produced by sanding and staining after the boards are laid. The second style is laminate flooring, not a modern technique, but a modern production process. Laminate flooring is a manufactured flooring whereby a veneered sheet of the timber of choice is glued to a supporting layer, or base, of medium- or high-density board. The cheaper versions may

have only a very thin veneer, and when used in a busy home where excessive wear is likely, their life can be reduced dramatically and, like some carpets, will require changing at regular intervals. The sheets are tongued and grooved, but as they vary in depth, and because they are not usually strong enough to walk on unsupported, they will require a secure base.

Making the choice between traditional and manufactured flooring will not be easy, and will depend upon what originally exists where the floor is going to be laid, and what effect is being created. Laying a traditional timber floor may well involve more building and constructional input when it is not only the floor covering but also part of the building fabric (although, like laminate flooring, traditional flooring can be laid on top of an existing base).

(opposite) **Elegance in generous room spaces.**

Memories of Goldilocks.

Wooden Floors

So, how do you choose between traditional and laminated? What are the key points to consider? In the end the answer will inevitably involve style and money. Laminated flooring is very effective, and starts at the lower end of the financial scale – though depending on the quality, it can also be very expensive; but it will be a long time before laminated flooring evokes the same feelings as traditional flooring. Traditional flooring will inevitably involve more work to install and to finish. The saying 'you only get what you pay for' may well be true – but in the end the choice is yours.

TRADITIONAL FLOORING

High quality, natural flooring has been used for centuries, and is now more in demand than ever before. A product of Mother Nature, a wooden floor can last a lifetime and gain in character over years of use; in fact it may even last longer than the house itself, so what you choose is very important.

In order to make the right selection there are certain significant factors to bear in mind. The first is the location of the floor: will it be exposed to exceptionally heavy traffic in, say, a hallway, or perhaps to the elements from external doors? Some timbers are better used

Mahogany overtones.

upstairs, rather than downstairs. The second significant factor is heating: is the house heated by a radiator system, or by an underfloor heating system? Advice from the supplier will help, though it is often considered that wider floorboards can be affected more by underfloor heating than the narrower boards. And the third significant point, but of no less importance, is whether the floor will be a prominent feature and a focus of attention, or simply a background for carpets and furnishings. Of course there are other factors, including cost and maintenance, but inevitably these are linked to the aforementioned points.

(opposite) North American maple.

All-round warmth and luxury.

Wooden Floors

The cost of a wooden floor can vary greatly according to the species of timber used; however, in general the requirements will inevitably remain constant, these being colour, wear resistance, durability and ease of maintenance.

Colour

The first and most common of these selection factors is colour. Everyone likes the look of a timber floor because floor timbers are just so beautiful, and they are available in whites and reds, even black, and almost every other shade and hue in between; so the number of possibilities for flooring is many and varied. Indeed for many, it is more than just a question of colour: the list of timber species conjures up romantic visions of woods and rolling countryside, in particular historically famous species such as oak and ash and pine. But these are just the tip of a very large iceberg, because there are other species of tree that are less well known but equally suitable for flooring, species such as merbau, kempas and jatoba. So whatever you choose, it is almost certain that you will not be disappointed.

Creating the right image.

(*opposite*) Limed oak boards.

English oak and limed oak complementing each

Wooden Floors

Getting the right formula.

WOODEN FLOORS
Because of the moisture content in wood it is likely that floors laid in winter will normally expand when summer arrives and the heating is turned off, and floors laid in the summer will contract when the heating is turned on.

Wear Resistance and Durability

The other important factors are wear resistance and durability, and these two points are closely linked. Traditional timber floors are available in such a range that it is almost impossible to list every type and how resistant they are to wear. The very best advice would be to visit the manufacturer or timber supplier, some of whom specialize in a single material, and others in several. Each timber will have advantages and disadvantages, and some will be more at home in one environment than others. The important thing is that you check the suitability of the timber against the environment in which it is to live.

Selecting a floor on the basis of technicality and science may be the practical thing to do, but for most people, the most important factor is appearance. Do you like what you see? From this point of view the selection process is simple: first choose the floor you like the look of, and then make sure it is suitable for your purpose. It really is as easy as that.

CARING FOR HARDWOOD FLOORS
• In areas adjacent to exterior doors use a protective mat to reduce damage from ground-in dirt.
• Always use felt protectors under the feet of tables, chairs and movable furniture. Change the pads regularly.
• Clean the floor regularly using a soft broom, or a vacuum cleaner with upholstery attachment.
• Always use cleaning products recommended by the manufacturers.
• Keep high heels in a good state of repair, or away from the floor.
• Keep water away from the floor. Wood and water do not mix well.
• Never place potted plants directly on the floor, even in dishes. Water can collect under the dish as a result of condensation and permanently mark the floor.
• Avoid exposing the wood to long periods of strong sunlight, as this will cause the wood to change colour. Move mats and furniture around to provide some shade.

Appalachian white oak.

Installation

Installing traditional wooden flooring may seem relatively easy, but it is a task that may in fact be fraught with problems, and it should only be undertaken by a professional. To achieve the best possible results the following points must be taken into consideration:

- location of the floor;
- age of the building;
- moisture content if the building is new;
- species of wood;
- method of heating;
- weather conditions at the time of fixing.

All these points will play an integral role in the success or indeed failure of the floor. Of course, traditional timber flooring can be used in almost all locations around the house, though extra precautions may be required where water is prevalent. Water and wood are not ready bedfellows, so the best advice is probably to keep the two as far apart as possible.

Wooden Floors

The conditions under which the floor is laid will differ from site to site, so first we will deal with new build. When the floor is being laid in a new building the two most important factors are humidity and moisture: the building must be 'in the dry', with windows and doors fitted, and all internal concrete should be dry long before the floor is laid. A good test for concrete is to lay a rubber car mat on it overnight, and if the patch is wet in the morning the concrete is still too wet. In the summer months the building must be well ventilated to reduce humidity and to allow it to dry out. In the winter months, when the building is sufficiently dry, the heating should be turned on and maintained at a level equivalent to the temperature required during occupancy. Where the floorboards are fitted to floor joists suspended over a concrete slab, ventilation will be required to allow a free flow of air through the void to prevent moisture build-up and therefore ideal conditions for mould and rot. The cross-ventilation will be maintained by using strategically placed air-bricks around the perimeter walls.

When the flooring is delivered it must be stored in the dry and, prior to fixing, the floor timbers should be unwrapped and placed in the rooms for which they are intended for at least five days; this will help them to acclimatize. Timber floors laid during the summer months are likely to expand, whereas floors laid in the winter months will contract, which is why acclimatization is so important.

Where the floor is laid in an existing dwelling the same terms apply, though not necessarily as stringently. The humidity and moisture content are important, though the ambient conditions are likely to be fairly constant in a home. Before laying the floor, the boards should be unwrapped and stored in the room for which they are intended.

The elegance of the Victorian era.

When the boards have fully acclimatized they can be fitted, and this is not a job for the inexperienced. There are so many 'tricks of the trade' with traditional timber flooring that only a professional will achieve the best results.

Underfloor Heating

With the introduction of new building requirements, designed to improve the insulation of ground floors, plus the advances made in underfloor heating methods, traditional timber flooring manufacturers have had to review their products to meet this demand. Heat and new wood do not go well together, the heat drying out the timber at a greater rate than may be required and inducing shrinkage.

Where underfloor heating is, or is going to be, the method of heating when the floor is laid, then this must be specified when the timber flooring is ordered, and the supplier/manufacturer must be made aware of this very important fact. He can then specify that the timber supplied is re-kilned to reduce the moisture content. Timber used for flooring is currently kiln dried to a standard humidity, and it is unlikely that this will be suit-

English and European oak.

able when used in conjunction with underfloor heating. In these circumstances there could be a high risk of damage as a result of shrinking and warping.

A supplier of floorboards kiln dried to only the standard humidity may specify that the boards should be just laid, and not nailed in position for a few weeks to allow shrinkage to take place. This is not the best advice, however, and is really not satisfactory for this type of heating, so it may be wise to approach an alternative supplier.

Where the underfloor heating is built into a floor screed, make sure that this is completely dry before laying the floor covering. If possible leave the heating on at the required room temperature for at least a couple of weeks before the floor is laid.

Character red elm.

Wooden Floors

North American elm.

Fixing

The three most common fixing methods for traditional flooring are secret nailing, gluing, and screwing and plugging. In secret nailing the board is nailed through the tongued joint of the tongued and grooved section and into the floor joist. The second is gluing, where a glue, recommended for this purpose, is fed along the grooved joint section before the joints are pushed together. Excess glue should be removed immediately with a damp cloth to avoid staining. The third method is screwing and plugging, which involves drilling holes, screwing through the boards into the floor joists, and then inserting a plug to conceal the hole. This is a very effective method, though time-consuming.

Expansion

Timber flooring is a natural product, so it is liable to movement, namely expansion and contraction across the length of the wood, or at 90 degrees to the grain. These movements may be small – how much will depend on the species of wood – but allowances must be made for them. When the floor is laid in a new house, a gap will be left around the perimeter walls to accommodate this movement. When the floor is laid in an existing house, the skirting boards must be removed and a gap left around the perimeter walls. The gap can then be concealed when the skirting boards are refitted.

Sanding (New Floor)

After the floor covering is in place and has been left for a couple of weeks to stabilize, it will need to be sanded down and sealed. Floorboards are available already sanded, but variances in thickness may leave undesirable high spots in the floor, so non-sanded floorboards may be a better choice.

To prepare the floor for sanding you must first sweep it clean, and then go

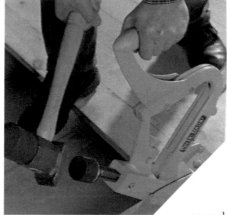

Hire a floor nailer to lay tongued and grooved floorboards.

round and make sure that all the nails are fully driven home. A high nail head will quickly demolish a sanding sheet.

To sand the floor you will require a professional drum-sanding machine; these can be hired, though a professional finish is usually only achieved by a professional. With the sander you will also require several sheets of sandpaper of varying grades, namely coarse, medium and fine. Always wear ear protectors and breathing masks during sanding.

Antique stone.

Wooden Floors

Fix the selected sandpaper to the machine and use according to instructions. After the first 'cut' use the 'edger' to sand around the edges, in corners, and in places the sander cannot reach. After drum-sanding the floor, repeat with a lesser grade sandpaper. Lastly, fill all holes and cracks in the floor surface, then finish with fine grade sandpaper. When the drum-sanding is completed, the floor can be hand scraped using a hand scraper, and sanded with a fine sandpaper and sanding block. Be sure to scrape sand in the direction of the grain.

Sanding (Old Floor)

Before sanding an existing floor, take professional advice to prevent damaging the floor beyond repair. Before you start, remove all the furniture, rugs, curtains and so on from the room, and if you are planning to decorate the walls or ceiling, do that before you start work on the floor. This will eliminate the possibility of spillage onto the floor, damaging or staining the surface.

When sanding an existing traditional floor, try to remove as little of the surface as possible. Sweep the floor clean, and make sure all nails are driven well below the surface, and all other high points are removed.

The coarseness of the sandpaper, and the number of passes needed by the drum sander to achieve the finish required, will depend upon the state of the floor. Where the surface is scarred and abused, just a few passes with coarse sandpaper will remove the old surface and achieve a smooth, blemish-free surface. Where the floor is in good or fair

American cherry.

condition, fewer passes and less-coarse sandpaper may produce the finish required.

Sealing

To protect the surface of the floor and allow for easy maintenance, the floor will need to be sealed; but before this sealing process, and before applying the finish to the floor, all of the construction work must be completed and the decorating finished. Selecting the type and grade of sealer you use on the floor will

Black walnut.

be governed largely by the location of the floor, by the amount of traffic it has to endure, and the type of finish you require. A hard gloss or matt finish can be achieved by using a lacquer or varnish, and this will provide a hard protective barrier against wear and tear. This hard finish will be durable and will flex with the floor, but when it is damaged it may be harder to repair than softer sealants. Water-based lacquers may be the best choice, as they are easy to apply and to maintain, and they will preserve the natural colour of the floor better than solvent-based sealers and oils.

If you want a softer finish, this can be achieved by using an oil-based sealant or a wax. These substances render the timber impermeable by blocking the pores, which eventually helps to produce the rich patina associated with traditional wooden floors.

Staining

Stain can be used when the colour of the timber differs from the colour you want. An oil-based stain and a sealer can be added together, and when applied to the floor will stain and seal in one application. Wax the floor to finish.

Bleaching

An increasingly popular style of floor decoration is bleaching; however, it should only be carried out in a well-ventilated area, and preferably by a professional. The bleaching process will lighten the floor colouring, when a white or pastel stain can be added for effect. Make sure the floor surface is free from oils and grease, and any other finish that might react with the bleach, creating an uneven effect. Before applying the

Bleached blue.

bleach to the new floor surface, be sure to test it first on a piece of waste floor timber. The bleaching process should be done only once.

Patina

The distinctive finish of a traditional timber floor is called the patina, and this can take years to achieve. Every three or four months apply a liquid wax to the floor using a mop or a soft cloth, polishing it off using the same utensil shortly afterwards.

LAMINATE FLOORING

Unlike traditional flooring, laminate flooring is a manufactured flooring product that has been around for about thirty years; however, it is only recently that it has grown in popularity as a floor covering. This method of replicating wood is the result of improved design and manufacturing techniques, ensuring that the life of a laminate floor now bears some resemblance to the outlay. Traditional wooden floors will always be in demand, but the cost, both financial and to the environment, can make quite a difference.

Laminate flooring originated in the countries of northern Europe and Scandinavia and has now grown worldwide, creating a huge market; there are countless styles and colours to choose from. The demand for this type of flooring, and the positive response from manufacturers, has ensured that the quality of the product will only improve, and that laminate flooring will grow as a major force

in floor coverings; it is certain to be around for a long time to come.

Typically, a sheet of laminate flooring will consist of an overlay, an image layer, a core board, a moisture barrier, and finally a sound-reduction underlay — though manufacturers will all vary in their methods of construction and the quality of each layer.

The overlay layer is the finished surface layer, the working surface, and it is the quality of this layer that will dictate the life expectancy of the floor. It must be durable and wear resistant, and to be of any use in the home it must be able to cope with the rigours of daily life,

First lay a suitable underlay.

Position the laminate boards leaving a gap around perimeter walls.

Wooden Floors

including traffic to and from rooms, children, pets, mud and cleaning. It must be scratch resistant, stain resistant, burn resistant and impact resistant. However, there has always been one element likely to cause this type of flooring irreparable damage, and that is water, excessive water causing the sheets to swell. Fortunately, manufacturers are now beginning to combat this problem, and some already offer life-time warranties on their products, including water or moisture warranties as well.

Below the surface layer of the laminate flooring is the 'image layer'. With the aim being to replicate the appearance of traditional flooring, this image layer will look like any of a number of species of wood, or even stone. And at almost no extra charge you can have a 'mixed' wood floor, including oak, ash and chestnut – the mixing possibilities are endless. You can even have replica stone or tile flooring. It is this range and adaptability that will encourage more and more people to

use this type of flooring as either the main floor or as a background for rugs and carpets.

The surface layer, or overlay, and the image layer can be classified as the 'front line' – but there is far more to laminate than just image. The board construction process, and this layer in particular, can be all that differentiates one manufacturer from another, and the life of one laminated flooring sheet as compared with another. Generally, this layer will

Making the home beautiful and cosy.

be medium- or high-density fibreboard (MDF or HDF), with low swelling characteristics. When you have selected the look you want, this is the important area to concentrate on, and some of the less expensive boards may not have the qualities you are looking for. 'Low-swelling', 'non-swelling' and 'swell resistant' are all terms used by the manufacturers, so check out warranties before you buy.

Further layers will again depend on

Lay the laminate boards, ensuring a tight fit.

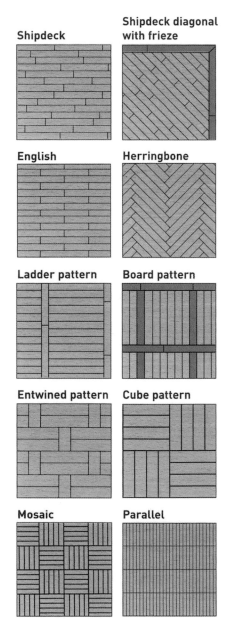

Shipdeck

Shipdeck diagonal with frieze

English

Herringbone

Ladder pattern

Board pattern

Entwined pattern

Cube pattern

Mosaic

Parallel

the quality of the board. A waterproof, or at least moisture-proof layer will be applied to all boards, and some will include a variety of sound-proof or insulating layers. These layers will add to thermal insulation, will reduce impact sound, and increase comfort for walking and standing on the floor.

In all, a sheet of laminate flooring is a fairly complex package, where selection should be made carefully, bearing in mind the room in which the flooring is going to go.

And finally, but just as important, laminate floors are easy to install: they have been designed for this purpose, and are being targeted at the do-it-yourself market, once again reducing the cost of this type of floor as compared to a traditional floor, and ensuring the longevity of the product. Of course, wood is here to stay – but it must be to the benefit of everyone that laminate flooring, with its versatility and good looks, is a very able substitute.

Installation

The process of installing a laminated floor has been designed for the do-it-yourself enthusiast, though you may want to use a professional; nevertheless, there are strict rules to be followed. The base on which the floor is to be laid, the preparations for the flooring, and the fixing method, are all points that need close consideration – but above all, follow the manufacturer's instructions.

A few laying patterns for parquet flooring.

Wooden Floors

A laminate floor is classified as a floating floor system, meaning that the floor sections are fixed together without being fixed to the sub-floor. Laid on a thin layer of insulation or underlay, it is the weight of the floor itself that holds it down. This is a further positive point, and dramatically reduces installment times.

When you have purchased your flooring, first unwrap it and place it in the room for which it is intended for at least a couple of days before installation, to allow the sheets to acclimatize.

The base floor must be level and clean. Laminate flooring can follow the contours of the base floor, so preparations to level it before the floor is laid must be sorted out. Most laminate floors have moisture barriers, and some have insulation barriers, and by following the manufacturer's instructions further layers – under-layers recommended by the manufacturer – can be installed on the floor area before the flooring is laid.

Parkett going bohemian on the Left Bank.

All skirting boards will need to be removed and architraves shortened. Around the perimeter of the room an expansion gap will be required to accommodate any movement in the flooring due to expansion or shrinkage. These movements may be as a result of changes in temperature or humidity, so the floor must be able to expand in all directions.

When all the preparations are complete, the floor can be laid fairly quickly. Glued or glue-less systems are available, and the latter can reduce the time spent laying the floor by quite a bit.

Once the floor is laid you should be able to walk on it immediately. Re-fit the skirting boards, and check that the doors clear the new floor level. Unlike a carpet where it doesn't matter if a door rubs against it, this will damage a laminate surface irreparably, so paring down the door will be a matter of utmost urgency.

Laminate flooring is extremely durable, but it is not indestructible, and the regular dragging of furniture, for instance, across the surface can scratch it and ruin the effect. Always lift such objects and carry them to a different position, and where possible, put felt pads under the feet of chairs and settees, and anything likely to damage the floor; protection is far better than repair.

PARQUET FLOORING

Parquet flooring is a quality product used to create quality floors, laid by professionals. Parquet or wood-block flooring consists of brick-like pieces of hardwood laid in a variety of patterns; unlike laminate flooring, each individual block is glued to the sub-floor, creating an interlocking, secure floor.

Parquet is not a manufactured product, though it does undergo a manufacturing process. It is solid wood, a completely natural material, and is available in a whole range of different woods, including oak, maple, cherry and beech.

Sustained durability, quality and choice.

The trees are cut from areas of sustainable and controlled forestry, and the wood is then stored in suitable conditions and dried before it is processed into blocks. A parquet floor is ideal for areas within the home where heavy traffic may be a problem; unlike laminate flooring, the surface can be sanded should damage occur.

When laying parquet, the sub-floor must be suitable for this purpose. It must be completely dry and free from irregularities likely to affect the evenness of the floor. Each individual wood block will be glued to the sub-floor using an adhesive recommended by the manufacturer. A parquet floor laid on top of floating insulation and creating a floating floor will not be glued to the insulation, but will be glued along adjacent edges and secured to adjacent wood blocks. After the floor is laid and before it is sealed it will be sanded, using the same method as for tra-

ditional floors, to remove uneven edges likely to cause people to trip.

Because parquet flooring is a completely natural product it creates a special floor of warmth and comfort; furthermore it is completely hygienic, offering no hiding place for pet allergens or dust mites. Parquet flooring is also suitable for use with underfloor heating.

After the parquet has been sanded and swept clean, it should be sealed using the same treatment as recommended for traditional floors, using a sealer recommended by the manufacturer. The routine care of parquet flooring should include keeping it clean and free from dirt and grit likely to scar or scratch the surface, and it should be kept free from excessive water likely to infiltrate the parquet blocks. Further protection can be afforded by adding self-adhesive felt pads to the feet of chairs, tables and other movable furniture.

Cork floor tiles fit the bill.

The warmth and protection of cork.

CORK

Cork bark is a completely natural and sustainable product removed from the cork oak tree every nine or so years, after which the bark renews itself. Removing the bark encourages re-growth and is not at all detrimental to the tree. For centuries the cork oak tree has been harvested for its bark, and it can be found in areas of Portugal, Spain and North Africa. The process of bark stripping is anything but fast: thus for the first stripping there is a wait of twenty-five or thirty years, and in the course of its life the cork oak will altogether produce only fifteen or so bark strippings.

Once the bark is removed it is reduced into small pieces; adhesive is added, and it is compressed into a mould to form the cork floor tiles we know today. This is not the only product cork bark is used for: it is also popular in the wine industry. When the cork blocks are set they are cut into tiles of regular shape, perfect for flooring. The quality of the cork tile can be checked in two significant ways: first its density – 450–500cu m/kg will be suitable for domestic flooring; and the second quality is the thickness of the finished tile.

Subtle tones of cork.

Cool elegance.

CORK TILES
• Where cork tiles are used in areas of heavy usage, they should be sealed with a clear pvc.
• Cork tiles are available in double size: 600mm x 300mm.
• Cork tiles are excellent with underfloor heating.
• Cork tiles are available in a range of colours suitable for domestic use.

Wooden Floors

Cork flooring has all the qualities of wood, being warm to the touch, durable, and with excellent insulation qualities; but unlike wood, cork can be used in bathrooms and kitchens. The tiles need to be secured to the floor using an appropriate and recommended adhesive, then sealed. A cork floor will not shrink or move in the way a traditional floor will move. In areas of high traffic this sealing process may be repeated every two or three years.

Cork tiles are available sealed with a varnish finish, pre-waxed and unsealed. The sealed tiles are suitable for use in domestic situations, though they will require further coats of acrylic varnish in areas where wear is heavy, and in bathrooms to completely seal the surface.

Pre-waxed tiles are ideal for areas where wear is less, such as bedrooms and bathrooms, but not kitchens. After the tiles are fitted they should be sealed using a recommended, good quality wax polish; in bathrooms this will seal the joints and resist water penetration.

Unsealed cork tiles can be used in any room, depending upon the quality of finish you apply. After laying the tiles the surface should be swept clean to remove dust and grit, then sealed using water or spirit-based varnish.

Cork tiles wear extremely well when properly sealed; they are also suitable in the presence of respiratory or allergen problems.

10 CARPETS

Floor coverings come in many shapes and sizes, with modern innovations and clever imitations chasing their market share – but the market leader, the one that is found in almost 90 per cent of the homes in the UK today, and with a history spanning possibly 2,000 years or more, is carpet. At first it was hand woven, now it is machine woven and, of course, the manufacturing process has improved beyond recognition with the introduction of machinery – but the end result has changed very little.

Oriental carpets were once the mark of pure luxury, the prized possessions of only the rich and famous. These fine carpets, handmade by nomadic tribesmen, came from far-away mystical places – Persia, Kashmir, Tashkent and Marakesh – each supplied with its own lurid tales of distant shores, crowded bazaars and child slavery.

Stocking the warehouse.

Twist pile, soft to touch and resilient.

Carpets

Several hundred years later, in the seventeenth century, a hundred years or so before the Industrial Revolution, the English carpet-making industry burst into life. And, like any other product with a history of its own, the humble carpet has its fair share of tales of skulduggery and intrigue, abduction, industrial espionage and adventure – though without, of course, heightening the senses or thrilling the emotions in the same way that gold and diamonds do.

As the demand for carpets increased, so the production techniques were also improved to meet it. Handmade carpets were soon made by machine, and when at last synthetics were introduced into the manufacturing process, a product that was once considered the prerogative of the privileged few became increasingly available to the masses. And it must be agreed that, given that nowadays very few homes in the UK use anything other than carpet as their main floor cov-

ering, this hard-earned outcome has been well worth the journey.

For the consumer the product is everything they wish for and more, with the plus points almost too many to list. But with flooring manufacturers pushing more and more innovative products into the marketplace, it is important to remember why the carpet industry has survived unchanged for so long. Of course the reason why someone buys a carpet will be different in every case, particularly in that carpets are available in an endless array of colours, designs and qualities to suit every need and every decorating scheme. Then there is the range of textures, making it the most luxurious of floor coverings, noiseless underfoot and a perfect sound barrier, creating both a sense of calm and a stress-free lifestyle. Or maybe it is because carpet is non slip, safe and warm to walk on, and gentle with children; or because it is relatively inexpensive and easy to install, unlike some modern floor coverings. Any or all of these may be the reasons why we prefer carpet in our homes, and why this type of floor covering is ideal for the modern home and the damp climate of the UK.

Berries with a twist.

(opposite) Honeycomb in Champagne.

Mosaic in Rye.

Carpets

Manufacture

Carpet manufacture has advanced through the ages and is now a flourishing, modern and high-tech industry; it has come a very long way from the Huguenot weavers from France and the introduction of the Jaquard 'card' method for introducing yarn to the loom. From a history filled with famous names such as Hargreaves, Arkwright and Watt, has grown an industry with few peers and a technologically advanced product.

There are two main types of carpet construction: woven and tufted, and non-woven. Woven carpets are formed where the structure of the carpet is held together as a result of the weaving process, the carpet pile loops woven into the backing material, then cut to form tufts. With non-woven carpets the carpet pile tufts are not woven into the backing material, they are secured with latex; a secondary backing is then added, for example hessian or foam.

Woven carpets – Axminster and Wilton are both famous household names – are manufactured using traditional weaving methods that tend to be slower and more labour intensive than

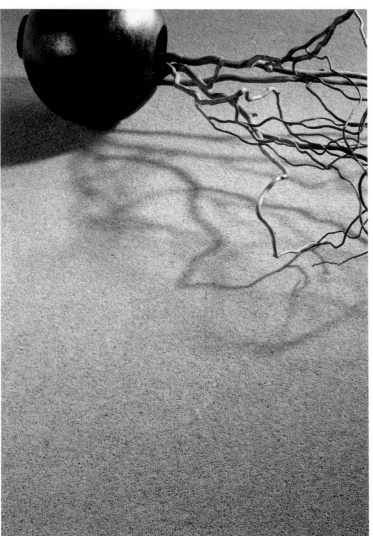

Moorland Heather Twist.

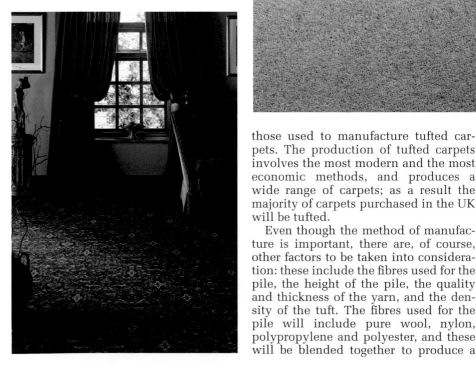

those used to manufacture tufted carpets. The production of tufted carpets involves the most modern and the most economic methods, and produces a wide range of carpets; as a result the majority of carpets purchased in the UK will be tufted.

Even though the method of manufacture is important, there are, of course, other factors to be taken into consideration: these include the fibres used for the pile, the height of the pile, the quality and thickness of the yarn, and the density of the tuft. The fibres used for the pile will include pure wool, nylon, polypropylene and polyester, and these will be blended together to produce a

Anatolian in Dark Damask.

yarn suitable for the carpet being made.

Wool has been used in the carpet industry for centuries and is often a home-grown product, though imports from New Zealand are also used. Wool is warm and soft to the touch, extremely resilient, does not soil easily, and is naturally flame retardant. Nylon is a synthetic polymer widely used in the textile industry. It is light, hard-wearing, responds well to stain-resisting treatments and has a high abrasion resistance. Polypropylene or olefin is stain resistant and has a high abrasion resistance, offering products that are very good value for money. Polyester is light and bulky and also offers very good stain-resistant qualities.

All these fibres are used in one blend or another; according to The Carpet Foundation, the blends most commonly used are these: 80 per cent wool – 20 per cent nylon; 80 per cent wool – 10 per cent nylon – 10 per cent polyester; and 50 per cent wool – 50 per cent polypropylene. These blends will determine the weight of the carpet and the pile density, which affect both appearance and performance and must be considered closely when purchasing a new carpet.

Torbay Country Weave.

Wisteria in Chinese Rose.

CHOOSING A CARPET

The single most important point to consider when choosing a carpet, and to ensure that you get the right one for the job, is where it will be located. Of course, all modern carpets are manufactured to be hard wearing and durable to a certain degree; however, you will find it pays to buy a better quality carpet for those areas that are subjected to excessive use. This is because, when you consider that, of the total floor area in a house, most of it is carpeted, you will realize how important carpet has become as a decorative item – so when a carpet becomes worn, this will seriously upset the decorative order of the house as a whole. It is this decorative part of the colour scheme that will be most affected, therefore, if you choose a carpet that is totally unsuitable for its location.

Once the location has been determined, which carpet you choose will then depend on three individual factors: the pile, the style and the colour. The pile is the soft surface of the carpet and includes twist pile, shag pile, velvet pile and saxony pile, each one suitable for a variety of locations around the home. The style may be plain or patterned; and the colour will be one of personal choice, so wide is the range currently available. A plain carpet will reputedly enlarge a room, giving it a feeling of space, whereas a heavily patterned carpet may have quite the opposite effect. Plain carpets, on the other hand, and in particular lighter plain carpets, are more likely to show marks than a patterned carpet.

(opposite) Barleycorn in Moorland Green.

100 per cent wool shag-pile carpets.

Carpets

The carpet you choose will also have an effect on the temperature of a room; thus where the room faces north, warm colours – oranges and reds – will brighten it up, and when it faces south, cooler colours such as blues and greens will cool it down. And then there is the choice of furniture and fabrics. A patterned carpet may give you a wider range to choose from when matching fabrics, while plain carpets appear to give furniture more space. In short, the list of requirements when choosing a carpet will be how suitable it will be for the location, how it will impinge on planned or existing colour schemes, and the furniture and what its life expectancy might be. All these points will then be governed by the budget available.

Preparations, Care and Maintenance

Fitting a carpet can easily fall into the category of do-it-yourself, even though carpet fitting is a skilled trade and requires specialist tools. Whether you use a skilled fitter or not, before laying the carpet always make sure the floor area is completely clean, and free from potentially damaging objects such as small stones and nails. Various jobs are

Moorland Heather.

Creating a sense of space.

best done before the carpet goes down: it is a good time to secure those annoying loose floorboards, and to install pipework, underfloor heating and insulation materials.

Each carpet should have an underlay. A good quality underlay will improve insulation and sound deadening, reduce heat loss and add to the acoustics. The method of securing the carpet may well depend on the manufacturer's recommendations, but will include the use of gripper rods, and also tack-less, tack-down and stick-down methods.

Carpets are available in a variety of widths to suit almost any room size, so where possible, joins are best avoided. If, however, joins are inevitable, a patterned carpet will need more care and attention to ensure the pattern is consistent and the carpet is laid the way you want it, so it is vital that you work with the fitter.

Once the carpet is fitted it should be vacuumed regularly to maintain its appearance. Initially this should be every day because of fluffing, then once a week except in areas where there is heavy traffic. Spots and spillages should be dealt with immediately. Use a cloth or kitchen roll in a dabbing motion to blot up liquid spills; remove solids using a

Moorland Heather Loop.

blunt knife. Always work from the outside in to avoid the spillage spreading, and use a dilute solution of carpet cleaner on the area to remove any signs from the carpet. Do not overwet the carpet, and always follow the manufacturer's instructions when dealing with stains and spills.

Every so often carpets should be given a thorough clean, and a good method is hot water cleaning. This is sometimes classified as steaming, and is particularly useful for removing ingrained particles and dirt. Use a rented machine, follow-

A plain carpet in a busy room.

Carpets

ing the instructions closely: a hot water and shampoo mixture is sprayed into the pile of the carpet, which traps the dirt particles; then, using the vacuum system, the water and dirt are sucked out together. Allow the carpet time to dry completely, and avoid walking on it, or repositioning furniture on it until it is.

CARPET TILES

Carpet tiles are an alternative to carpet, and they are easy to fit. Heuga carpet tiles are particularly popular, and are manufactured from either 100 per cent polypropylene, 100 per cent nylon, or 80 per cent polypropylene and 20 per cent recycled nylon. These tiles are extremely hard wearing, they are suitable for any room in the house, and they do not require an underlay. Often loose laid, the appearance and performance of carpet tiles will depend on how they are laid, and the quality of the surface on which they are laid.

Before laying carpet tiles, first make sure the floor is clean, dry and level; remove all old, damaged and uneven floor coverings, and make sure the surface is free from grease, paint and oil. When laying carpet tiles on uneven wooden flooring, a base layer of plywood or hardboard would be advisable – though hardboard should be dampened a day before the tiles are laid to prevent expansion. Carpet tiles should not be laid on solid floors with no damp-proof membrane.

Each carpet tile will have an arrow on its reverse side showing the direction of the pile lay. To avoid shading problems as a result of pile direction, the tiles should be laid with the arrows in alternate directions. Carpet tiles can be loose laid butted closely together for a tight fit; every fifth row should be secured to the sub-floor with double-sided tape to stabilize the floor covering and restrict movement of the tiles; so, too, should the cut tiles round the perimeter of the room.

Carpet tiles do not require special maintenance; regular vacuum cleaning will help maintain appearance, and they can be easily replaced when a tile is damaged or stained. The extensive range of tiles available will make designing and planning a floor scheme easy.

Antique Splendour Ling.

Folkweave in Champagne.

Antique Splendour Rustic Dawn.

FROM FLEECE TO FLOOR: MAKING AXMINSTER CARPET

There is really nothing quite like the warm and luxurious feel of a pure new wool carpet with its soft and springy fibre. It will retain its colour and beauty for years, and although there have been many attempts to duplicate its unique properties, there is still nothing quite like pure new wool. Nowhere is this better known than at Axminster in the heart of the Devonshire countryside, where a world-famous, world-class industry has grown up over the last 250 years in the manufacture of 100 per cent pure wool and, more recently, wool-rich carpets.

On a midsummer's day in 1755 a cloth weaver local to the town of Axminster wove his first carpet by hand, and it was subsequently named after the local market town where he lived and worked. Slow and laborious progress over the years has resulted in what is now described as the finest spinning and dyeing mills in the country.

So how is a pure new wool carpet made? Well, at the heart of the business is the wool of Axminster's own flock of purebred Drysdale sheep, particularly favoured for its hard-wearing qualities, and which, when blended with wool from other breeds, produces the very finest yarn: this is what is used in the production of the Axminster carpets.

The wool to blend with the Axminster wool is bought by buyers who regularly attend wool auctions held by the British Wool Marketing Board, which handles the fleece wool grown in the UK on behalf of the 80,000 sheep farmers. There are well over 40 million sheep in Britain, and more pure breeds than in any other country, and two thirds of the wool produced is used in quality carpet manufacture.

The raw wool purchased by the buyers is then shipped to Buckfast Mill, on the southern edge of Dartmoor, where it is sorted according to fibre length and colour. White wool will be dyed in lighter colours or left natural, tinted fleeces in darker colours. To begin the process the wool fleeces are mechanically stretched out, or 'opened', to a more

Tiling to a theme.

Lay carpet tiles according to the arrows.

All-round quality.

Carpets

uniform mass, and then blended together to provide the most suitable mix of wool for carpet weaving. They are then subjected to a six-stage washing process to remove dirt, grease and other impurities, using the clean water from the crystal-clear streams of Dartmoor.

The wool is then dried, and any dust is extracted; next, the wool is blown into large storage bins where it is allowed to relax in order to regain its original structure. It is then lightly lubricated, baled, and left to condition before the next process – carding.

Carding is a precisely monitored operation using a series of progressively more finely spiked rollers to comb out the wool fibres into a fine, uniform web. Carried along an array of narrow conveyor belts, the layer of wool is divided into narrow strips, or 'slubbings', that are rolled into fragile strands before being loaded onto the spinning frame. The fragile slubbings are then spun at more than 5,000rpm into a single-ply yarn.

By twisting the strands together as two or more ply, additional strength and density is acquired by the yarn, affecting the eventual weight and quality of the finished carpet. The yarn is then wound into shanks before it is given a final washing to enhance the dyeing technique.

To produce the delicate shades and colours required, colourfast dyes are used, with the composition of the dye, its temperature and the immersion time of the hanks all being closely monitored, using a computerized system that ensures precise matching of the colours. The hanks are then rotated in a hydro-extraction unit to remove any excess moisture before they pass through an electronically controlled steam-drying process to ensure uniformity of moisture content.

Once dried, the hanks are allowed to cool and condition naturally, before being wound onto more manageable 'cones' and packaged for despatch to the carpet-weaving looms. Several thousand kilos of yarn make this same journey every day.

New carpet designs are developed on computer, where pattern and colour ideas can be visualized and changed to meet the requirements of the customer or designer. The more modern looms will be directly linked to the design com-

Carding.

Spinning into yarn.

Twisting.

puter, where tuft colours are selected to form a configuration and provide the perfect solution for weaving one-off bespoke designs. The more traditional and familiar designs are transferred to mechanical templates called 'jacquard' cards. The 'jacquard' card was first invented by

Designing by computer.

A loom at work.

Inspecting the carpet.

Joseph Jacquard in 1801 and represented a major step forward in the carpet-making process. It is a process still widely used today, and works on the same principle as that used to create mechanical organ music. The machine-readable array of holes in the jacquard card represents the colour of each single carpet tuft and several hundred of these cards are laced together to form each carpet design.

The incoming cones of yarn are then subjected to inspection and colour comparison before being rewound onto smaller bobbins, which are in turn placed on a feed array for the loom called a 'creel'. Up to 12,000 bobbins in a creel can feed a single loom.

Part of the base of the carpet is the jute 'weft', grown and spun in Bangladesh. The weft is passed between alternate parallel cotton yarns or 'warps'. The yarn is fed into carriers controlled by the jacquard. A colour is selected by the jacquard, which causes the corresponding yarn to be offered up by the carrier to the gripper. The grippers then draw the pre-selected lengths of yarn, which are cut by a series of knives. The resulting tufts are positioned between the warps by the grippers, and retained by each pass of the weft. In this way the lattice of tightly packed cords and wool tufts builds up to form a carpet, at the rate of 3–5yd per hour, all under the expert supervision of a weaver. The quality of the finished carpet will be determined by the number of tufts there are per square inch, the count or weight of the yarn, and the length of the pile.

The newly woven carpet is now lightly brushed, then gently steamed, before tip shearing removes any high points in the pile to give it a smooth, level finish. At this stage any minor faults will be corrected by hand in a way that replicates the weaving process; it then moves on to large passing tables for inspection and further correction if required.

The carpet is brushed again to remove any foreign matter, and squared for alignment and symmetry. After further steaming to burst open the lush woollen pile, a coating of vinyl is applied to the back of the carpet to assist tuft retention and to ease cutting and fitting.

Carpets

Finally, following a meticulous examination on a specially illuminated tilting table, the finished carpet is given a bar code identification to ensure traceability of the carpet's processes before it is dispatched to the warehouse where carpets are cut and sized to order requirements.

Steaming the carpet.

CARPET CARE
• Carpets should be vacuumed regularly to remove any dirt and grit particles likely to damage the pile. Where traffic is high, the carpet should be vacuumed on a daily basis; for medium traffic areas, twice a week; and the entire house once a week.
• Change the vacuum bags regularly, and check the beater bars for objects that may damage the surface of the carpet.
• Rugs can be placed in areas of high wear; where strong sunlight can fade the colours, these rugs should be removed and cleaned regularly. Furniture coasters should be used under castors.
• Carpets should be cleaned using a professional cleaner every eighteen months to two years, taking particular care in areas of heavy usage.

Everything seems so natural.

11 NATURAL FIBRES

For centuries natural fibres, in the form of rush matting, have been used as a floor covering, and even as a bedding, in and around central Asia, southern Europe, North Africa and North and South America. There are also many examples of their increasing use in the UK at around the turn of the last century. Then, just as demand was beginning to gather pace and a serious interest was being shown in this type of floor covering by home furnishers, the introduction of man-made synthetic fibres seriously changed the floor-covering landscape. With such masses of colour and ready availability, this new product achieved monumental status almost overnight, and sales began to rocket. Thankfully, however, this was only a short flourish – although for the natural fibre stockists and manufacturers it also proved to be a time of reckoning.

Their product had been exposed as having distinct and inherent limitations in colour and texture, and as a result of limited availability, could not be competitive on price – but time would reveal that these were not the only qualities that a prospective buyer would be looking for. Natural fibre products had their own qualities, but the passage of time has provided another ingredient that the fast-track manufacturers could not buy or easily reproduce. It is a third world, almost medieval quality associated with stone walls, oak beams and thatched roofs: it is *style*.

The demand for synthetics had reached the heights and then levelled off, and in a world where environmental issues are foremost, this tried and tested material, handcrafted by man and with its natural qualities, began a comeback. Now the signs are extremely promising, and the future looks particularly bright.

Alternative flooring where excellence comes naturally.

Natural Fibres

Manufacturers using natural fibres have addressed the 'colour' issue without impinging on quality, and designers and specifiers are once again extolling the virtues of this purely natural product; it can look spectacular in a modern home or in a country cottage, and in any room of the house.

The natural fibre floor coverings of today are just the same as they were centuries ago, but without the shortcomings. Originally, because of its instant availability, this type of floor covering would have been replaced and re-laid at will. Today, with the use of modern production techniques, natural fibre floor coverings can compete with others of the best quality, combining a unique quality with a love of nature.

There are around forty different types of natural fibre used for weaving, though not all meet the stresses and strains of the modern home. The fibres that have

Alternative flooring.

Sisal Super Panama.

134

Sisal in mulberry.

proved to be up to the task are coir, sisal, seagrass and jute. Bamboo is becoming increasingly common, though I feel this is more of a 'wooden' floor covering than a natural fibre one.

These well known natural fibres have a long historical background. Coir, for example, possibly originated in areas of the western Pacific and is now found growing in India, Malaysia, East and West Africa, and Central and South America. Reportedly spread between continents on ocean currents, the use and abilities of coir have been written about for over three thousand years. Sisal originated in Central America and Mexico, and was later introduced to East Africa in the belief that it was a crop ideal for their conditions, though the majority of sisal production is now attributed to Tanzania: it is an on-going localized industry benefiting local growers.

YARNS

Natural fibres, just like any material used in the manufacture or making of carpets, are only as good as the raw materials from which they are made, and the quality of the construction process. The raw fibre is first spun into a yarn, and is then woven into the finished carpet with, generally, a latex backing.

WEAVES

There are several weaves in use today, the most popular for domestic situations being 'bouclé', Panama and herringbone:

Sisal – bouclé.

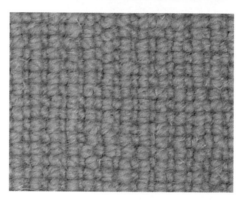

All-wool – bouclé.

Jute – bouclé.

All-wool – bouclé.

(far left) All-wool natural carpet.

Seagrass – basketweave.

• Bouclé is the heaviest and most hard-wearing weave, with a ribbed appearance creating a traditional look.
• Panama has a traditional-style weave particularly suitable for domestic locations.
• Herringbone has a traditional zig-zag weave, offering a different and distinctive effect.

(far left) Jute – herringbone.

(left) Coir – superior/sisal weft.

(far left) Seagrass – natural.

(left) Seagrass – superior.

(far left) Sisal – super panama.

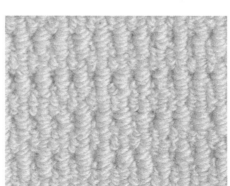

(left) All-wool – textured.

Natural Fibres

COIR

Coir is best described as the fibrous material that protects coconuts. A coconut is the seed of the coconut palm tree, and it grows inside a much larger 'husk'. This husk has a leathery skin, and it is between the husk and the coconut that coir is found, its purpose being to act as a shock absorber when the coconut husk falls from the tree. Coconut palms can be found in areas where the humidity is high and there is plenty of fresh water, conditions often to be found along seashores, conjuring up memories of tropical islands.

Coconut husks.

The coconut 'husk' is produced when the flower of the coconut palm is pollinated, and it takes approximately a year to develop completely. Harvesting the husk can be difficult, so much so that in areas surrounding Thailand and Indonesia monkeys have been trained to climb the trees and remove and loosen the husks. The coconut is then separated from the husk, a process known as 'dehusking', carried out by driving the husk onto a sharp spike. The coconut is removed, and the remaining husk is then soaked in sea water; this causes the fibres to swell and soften before they are removed and spun into yarn.

The fibres can be spun into a variety of designs, including ones with a natural and a bleached finish. Coir is ideal for 'busy' areas: it is strong and will readily cope with the wear and tear of modern life.

Coir, a highly textured finish, able to withstand all the wear and tear of modern life.

SISAL

Sisal is a product of the leaves of the *Agave sisalana* plant, from which it gets its name. It is best described as the toughest of the natural fibres, and as a result of this strength and durability it is traditionally used in making both rope and floor coverings. The *Agave* genus of plant is primarily a desert-type plant with long, narrow, succulent leaves that finish in a sharp point. During the growing process, and after several of these leaves are produced, a long, pole-like, flower-bearing stalk develops. This stalk can sometimes exceed 20ft (6m) in height. When flowering is complete, the plant dies. To harvest it, several of the leaves will be removed for sisal production, while ensuring that enough are left to support the growing process of the plant and the production of bulb-like shoots for future propagation and the next season's sisal plant.

Agave sisalana.

After the leaves are removed they are crushed and scraped, and the fibres removed; these are then washed, dried and graded before being spun into yarn. This yarn is not only very strong, but also soft and supple enough to be woven by machine. Like coir, sisal is available in several different weaves and a limited range of colours, each selected to show the natural qualities of the fibre.

Sisal, an organic fibre, makes a beautiful and strong floor covering.

139

SEAGRASS

As the name suggests, seagrass carpets are constructed from grass soaked in sea water, this being an integral part of its production. Traditionally, seagrass is grown in the paddy fields of China; when it is ready for harvesting, the paddy fields are flooded with sea water. The grass is then harvested, dried, and spun into a yarn before weaving. The yarn is strong, and ideal for the manufacture of floor coverings. The fibre construction of seagrass makes it difficult to dye, so it is often available in its natural state, with all the inconsistencies of colour that are part of its attraction.

Seagrass carpets are available in both natural and herringbone weaves, and are not really suitable for use in kitchen or bathroom areas.

Seagrass, grown in Chinese paddyfields.

Seagrass is inherently strong and resistant.

JUTE

Jute is the product of the genus *Corchorus*, a herbaceous annual, and is grown in the warm and humid regions of Asia, including India and Bangladesh. This woody herb is grown to a height of up to 9ft (nearly 3m), when it is hand harvested; it is then soaked in water, and pounded to release the fibres found in the inner balk. These fibres are then washed and dried, and finally spun to produce a silky soft and lustrous yarn.

Jute is a fine natural fibre that looks great and feels good. However, it is possibly not best suited for kitchens and bathrooms, nor for areas of heavy traffic such as hallways. Jute is available in a variety of weaves, including bouclé and herringbone, and it makes a superb floor covering.

Genus *Corchorus.*

WOOL

Wool is the most common of all natural fibres and has been used for centuries in the manufacture of floor coverings.

Unlike mass-produced carpet manufacture, natural fibre wool carpets are made in the traditional way, using a flat weave process. The raw wool is first spun into a

Jute, harvested by hand and dried in the sun.

141

single yarn, then two or more of these are twisted together to produce a yarn of the strength required, and capable of being woven. The yarn can be mixed with sisal, linen or jute to add an additional texture.

INSTALLATION

Natural fibre floor covering may not be cut in the same way as traditional floor coverings, so the services of an experienced fitter are strongly recommended; note, however, that the cost of installing a natural fibre carpet may be higher than with standard fitted carpets.

Natural fibre carpets perform better when stuck to a dry surface, either the main sub-floor, or to a secure underlay. Wool carpets can also be fitted using the conventional gripper method. Natural fibres absorb moisture and tend to expand and contract according to atmospheric conditions, so for reasons of stability, the floor covering should be stuck down.

After purchasing the floor covering, in the first instance it should be stored in the room for which it is intended for at least two days. Then the floor covering can be stuck to the clean, dry sub-floor, or to a suitable and recommended underlay. The use of an underlay will soften the carpet and add both insulation and sound-deadening qualities to the floor area.

AFTER CARE

Because natural fibre carpets have a latex backing, the build-up of dirt beneath the floor covering is greatly reduced. Regular cleaning with a vacuum will reduce any build-up, and any spills — whether they are likely or not to cause stains — should be cleared up immediately. Cleaning products should be chosen that are suitable for the particular natural fibre, and only used according to the manufacturer's recommendations.

ALLERGIES
Many allergists recommend a central vacuum system, because it eliminates the recirculation of germ-laden air and dust. All the unhealthy air is vented outside, and the dirt is collected in a large bin and emptied every three or four months.

Wool, natural tones and natural weaves.

12 VINYL

Vinyl began to play a major role in domestic flooring in the 1960s as an alternative to linoleum, and after years of improvements and creativity since that time, it is now a leading player in this field. No other floor covering offers the same range of colours and styles as vinyl, or has the ability to replicate a look or a texture in quite the same way. Add to this the manufacturing advances in resilience, and in wear and stain resistance, and this is a product suitable for almost every location and every situation.

The manufacture of vinyl can vary, though the structure is basically the same. There are three definite layers in domestic sheet vinyl: the top, or wear layer, a central core, and a base layer that is often felt-backed. The most commonly used method of manufacturing domestic vinyl floor coverings is with the use of a rotogravure printing process: this produces what is known as 'rotogravure vinyl'. During this process, the central

Onyx Grey Marble vinyl flooring.

Ceramic tiles and vinyl flooring.

core of the vinyl, the gel coat, is passed under a revolving cylinder that prints the pattern onto the gel coat. A clear wear layer is then applied to the surface of the gel coat. This clear wear layer is critical to the performance of the vinyl, and will determine its resilience and durability. How thick it is will vary from one manufacturer to another, and will ultimately determine the life of the vinyl flooring. The more expensive vinyl flooring will generally have a thicker wear layer and ultimately a longer life; furthermore, with such rapid improvements in structure and design, the more expensive vinyls will clearly be expected to outperform those vinyls at the cheaper end of the scale.

Of course, vinyl flooring is not a natural product, it is manufactured – though it is often very difficult to spot the replica. Vinyl has other qualities in that it is easy to clean and to install, it retains its shape, and it is unlikely to be affected by atmospheric conditions; on the down side, direct sunlight over a long period may fade the colours. In short, vinyl has a great number of

advantages, and very few disadvantages. It is also available in sheet form, and as rigid tiles.

As versatile as your imagination.

INSTALLATION

The installation of vinyl flooring will follow the same procedure as carpets and wood laminates. However, note that vinyl will follow the contours of the base sub-floor more closely than carpet or wood, so be sure to clean and level the sub-floor thoroughly where necessary. If the floor is too uneven for a proprietary levelling compound to resolve, then an underlay of plywood can be fitted. One of the mistakes most commonly made when fitting vinyl flooring is not levelling the floor properly.

American oak vinyl flooring.

Natural-looking clay
quarry vinyl flooring.

Vinyl

First, remove all the furniture from the room, and where possible remove the skirting boards and architraves. When flooring a bathroom, try to remove the toilet, the wash hand-basin pedestal and the bath surrounds as well: this will make cutting easier, and any errors can be hidden under the repositioned units. Where possible, all obstructions should be removed and refitted after the vinyl is laid.

Clean the floor thoroughly using a broom or a vacuum cleaner, removing all dirt particles or flooring irregularities likely to damage the vinyl. A light liquid cleaner can then be used to remove any oil or grease likely to react against the adhesive. Doors may require adjustment or shortening, and it may be possible to do this without removing them using special tools; alternatively remove the door, cut it down and refit it when the vinyl is laid. Check closely that the bottom of the door has sufficient clearance over the vinyl so as not to mark it when it is opened and closed.

Platinum Pearl Molten vinyl flooring.

CARING FOR VINYL FLOORING

• The surface layer, or wear layer, of vinyl sheet and vinyl tiles is designed to protect the pattern layer against wear and tear; however, it can be damaged, and when it is, it is difficult to repair.

• The surface can be protected by fitting felt pads to movable furniture, including tables and chairs. Also, never drag anything, even a vacuum cleaner, across the vinyl floor.

• Heavy furniture with castors should be moved very carefully, possibly on strips of carpet, to reduce the risk of grooving the floor.

• Dirt and grit should be removed at once to reduce the risk of scratching.

• Vinyl should be cleaned regularly using a soft broom or a vacuum cleaner with an upholstery nozzle fitted.

• Only use recommended cleaning fluids, and apply them according to the manufacturer's recommendations.

• Vinyl flooring can discolour or fade as a result of strong, direct sunlight, so place rugs and suitable curtains or blinds at points of high risk.

• Hot objects will damage the surface and must be kept off the vinyl.

• Where the vinyl is used adjacent to exterior doors a mat or rug should be used to reduce wear and tear.

• Stiletto and high-heeled shoes, especially those where the heel is in need of repair, will damage a vinyl floor surface and should be taken off.

• Rubber-backed and non-ventilated rugs should be avoided, though all rugs and mats should have a non-slip backing to avoid accidents.

Where sheets must be cut and joined, make sure the pattern works properly, and runs in the required direction, before either cutting or fixing the flooring; also that the seam area is clean and dry, so the adhesive holds the seams properly.

When you have familiarized yourself with the room layout, and if there is a seam, mark the seam line before laying the adhesive, and fit the smallest section of vinyl first. Trowel down the adhesive using the recommended tools, and apply according to the manufacturer's recommended instructions. Where there is a seam, extra careful attention will be required to ensure a very tight contact, otherwise dirt can build up and highlight the join. When the work is finished, the floor can then be rolled with a heavy roller to remove all air bubbles and ensure a good bond with the adhesive.

Once the floor is laid the only treatment required will be a very light wash with a damp mop.

After installation try not to walk about on the floor, and avoid seamed areas for

African slate vinyl flooring.

a couple of days – and definitely do not move any furniture. A 'must do' is to

Iced glass vinyl flooring.

147

keep the room temperature at the normal level, as this allows the adhesive to cure properly. Also, after the floor covering is laid and ready to walk on, be careful that furniture with casters or rollers does not mark the floor surface: use the special cups that are made specifically to reduce point loads on this type of flooring. The legs of tables and chairs can be fitted with felt pads for the same reason.

Follow the same procedure when installing rigid tiles, though there will be a lot more seams to worry about. Lay out the floor area in the same way that you would lay out ceramic tiles, allowing for a continuity of pattern, and familiarize yourself with any permanent obstructions. Then mark a centre line in the room taken from both sets of opposite walls, and always work from this centre line. Apply the adhesive correctly and to the manufacturer's instructions, making sure not to apply too much or too little, or over too large an area. Fit the tiles firmly and securely, making sure every seam is a tight fit: gaps will attract dirt, and may cause the corners of the tiles to raise. Remove all waste adhesive from the surface of the tiles before it dries.

Use the same care and cleaning techniques recommended for sheet vinyl flooring.

Checks and balances.

13 LINOLEUM

After suffering what could only be considered a mid-life crisis in the 1960s, linoleum floor covering is now making a sustained domestic and commercial recovery. In much the same way as natural floor coverings fell out of favour, and possibly as a direct result of the introduction of synthetically manufactured carpets, linoleum sales also fell off dramatically. Now there is a marked resurgence in linoleum sales as a new generation of flooring buyers consider their options, and find this one-time low-cost material has many attributes and few drawbacks.

The history of this extremely popular floor covering and its nearest predecessors goes back to the manufacturing of floorcloths, in Scotland, in the 1840s. In the manufacture of floorcloth, which was based on similar principles to linoleum, canvas was stretched over wooden frames, and coats of size, a thin soap-like liquid, were spread on to seal the canvas; then layers of a treacly paint were added.

Each layer was allowed to dry before another was added, the topside receiving more layers than the underside. To finish off, the sheets were sent to the printing building where a decorative finish was added.

Luxuriously understated.

A choice of colours and moods.

Linoleum

The original linoleum floor covering was patented by Frederick Walton in the 1860s, as a replacement to a rubber composite floor covering called Kamptulicon. With the main ingredient being linseed oil, the name 'linoleum' evolved from the Latin for linseed, *linum*, and *oleum*, for oil. The oil is boiled, then mixed with melted resins, powdered wood and/or cork, ground limestone drying agents and pigments, and is fixed to a jute backing layer. This mixture is formed into a durable sheet by applying heat and compression. Linoleum is made largely from natural and renewable raw materials that make it environmentally friendly.

Linoleum is primarily available in roll form, approximately 6ft 6in (2m) wide and up to 98ft (30m) in length, though some manufacturers are also offering large squares of linoleum, starting at 13sq ft (1sq m). The original linoleum was available in a wide variety of printed designs, with replicas of wood grain, stone and ceramic tile amongst the most popular choices. Today's linoleum offers an extensive range of colours and effects suitable for almost any location or situation (though it is often suggested that linoleum is not recommended in bathrooms). The benefits of linoleum are as follows:

- Hygienic and easy to clean;
- Naturally antibacterial;
- Resistant to fading;
- Flame retardant;
- Naturally anti-static;
- Resistant to grease and oils;
- Suitable for use with underfloor heating;
- Biologically degradable;
- Anti-slip;
- Warm underfoot.

SEASONING BLOOM

There is a natural occurrence in the manufacturing process of linoleum that leaves a yellow film on the linoleum during the drying process: this is known as 'seasoning bloom', and it will be more or less noticeable depending upon the colour of the linoleum. Blues and greens appear greener, while beige looks more yellow, and it is not visible at all on yellows and reds. This film is only temporary and will disappear when exposed to light, although it may take hours in light buildings, or even weeks in dark buildings, to complete the process. The application of protective floor polishes will not stop the process, but it may slow it down.

A warm contemporary touch.

Clean lines making a
statement.

151

Linoleum

INSTALLATION

Before fitting linoleum sheet, make sure the sub-floor is smooth, dry and clean, and free from paint, oils, solvents and any other foreign matter. Where there is grease or oil likely to react against the adhesive, this can be removed using a suitable liquid cleaner. Store the new rolls of linoleum and the adhesives in the room where the floor is to be laid for at least two days before installation to allow them to condition at room temperature.

Remove all furniture and check the door levels. Where doors require adjustment or shortening this may be possible without unhanging the door using special tools designed for this purpose, or by removing the door, cutting it down and refitting it when the linoleum sheet is laid. Check closely that the bottom of the door has sufficient clearance over the floor covering so as not to mark it when the door is opened and closed.

Where there will be joins in the

linoleum sheet, make sure the pattern works properly before cutting the sheets, and also make sure the seam area is clean and dry so the adhesive will hold the seams properly. Check that the pattern runs in the required direction before either cutting or fixing the flooring, and keep the rolls with the face side out, ready to begin installation. Make sure that any seams do not coincide with seams in the sub-floor, if it is timber sheeting; the seams should be at least 6in (150mm) apart.

When you have familiarized yourself

A look that fits anywhere.

As versatile as your imagination.

with the room layout, and if there is a seam, mark the seam line before laying the adhesive, and fit the smallest section first. Trowel down the adhesive using the recommended tools, and apply it according to the manufacturer's recommended instructions. Where there is a seam, be extra careful to ensure a very tight contact, otherwise dirt can build up and highlight the join. When complete, the floor can be rolled with a heavy roller to remove all air bubbles and ensure a good bond with the adhesive. Clean residue adhesive from the surface using a clean white cloth dampened with water.

Once the floor is laid, the only treatment required will be a very light wash with a damp mop.

Warning: Linoleum can increase slightly in width and reduce in length as a result of contact with the wet adhesive. To reduce this risk and compensate for any movement, installation must be carried out according to the recommended installation procedures supplied.

Simply stunning.

Creating the right impressions.

Linoleum

After installation, try not to walk about on the floor, and avoid seamed areas for a couple of days – and definitely do not move furniture. Also keep the room temperature at the normal level, as this allows the adhesive to cure properly. Furniture with casters or rollers may mark the floor surface, so use the special cups made to reduce point loads on this type of flooring. Tables and chairs can be fitted with felt pads for the same reason.

PRODUCT GUIDE

The following guide has been prepared to compare and rate the range of domestic floor coverings currently available and in everyday use. These ratings may vary from manufacturer to manufacturer and are assessed on best quality.

All the ratings are based on standard domestic situations with dry, clean sub-flooring. Fade Resistance is based on resistance to direct sunlight. Wood is pre-finished solid wood flooring, not unfinished.

	Stone	Wood	Laminate	Cork	Carpet	Natural Fibres	Vinyl	Linoleum
Damage Resistant	4	3	3	3	3	3	2	2
Moisture Resistant	5	4	2	4	2	2	5	3
Stain Resistant	4	4	5	4	2	2	5	5
Fade Resistant	5	4	4	4	4	3	5	5
Ease of Cleaning	5	4	5	5	2	2	5	5
Healthy Flooring	5	5	5	5	2	3	5	5
Suitable for Underfloor Heating	5	5	5	5	5	5	5	5
Ease of Repair	2	3	1	3	2	1	1	1

Ratings: (1) Very poor   (2) Poor   (3) Average   (4) Good   (5) Very good

GLOSSARY OF TERMS

Adhesives Used for bonding the floor covering to the sub-floor according to the manufacturer's recommendations.

Building paper A vapour barrier of paper with a bitumen layer; it is available in rolls, and does not sweat like a polythene sheet.

Burrs Clusters of small knots found in wood.

Checks and shakes Small, non-structural surface cracks found in wood.

Crazing A feature of many glazed tiles caused by temperature changes.

Ends matched Where the boards are tongued and grooved on the ends as well as along their length.

Expansion gap The gap left around the perimeter of the room to allow for any expansion.

Fading Where carpets are subjected to varying degrees of UV rays and direct sunlight.

Floating floor A floor not fixed directly to the sub-floor.

Hardwood Timber taken from a deciduous tree and not necessarily based on the hardness of the wood.

Humidity The amount of water vapour in the air.

Inlays Smaller pieces of wood introduced to create a decorative effect, around borders for example.

Insets Small decorative pieces inlayed into the main floor

Kiln drying A process where the moisture content of the timber is reduced to ensure stability.

Knots Found in wood where small and large branches stemmed from the main trunk. Can crack during kiln drying.

Ledging Where one side of a vinyl sheet or linoleum seam overlaps another.

Moisture content The amount of water remaining in the timber; it will change with the temperature and humidity of a room.

Movement The natural changes in timber as a result of temperature and humidity in the room.

Natural fibres Grown naturally; includes grasses and wool.

Nap A soft downy surface; the pile.

Patina A gloss produced naturally when wood ages.

PVC Polyvinyl chloride, a widely used plastic with many applications.

Sealer A water- or spirit-based coating applied to the floor to enhance the colour and protect the surface.

Secret nailing A method of fixing the flooring by driving the nails in at 45 degrees through the tongue of the tongue-and-groove flooring.

Shedding Newly fitted carpets 'shed' or 'fluff'.

Suberin The inherent substance of cork, a natural insect repellent.

Underfloor heating Where the heat source is installed beneath the floor covering.

Underlayment A sheet material laid on the substrate beneath the flooring material.

Underglazed Where no glazing or any other coating has been applied.

LIST OF SUPPLIERS

The publisher wishes to thank the following suppliers for their kind permission to reproduce their photographs and information in this book.

BUILDING PRODUCTS

Ardex UK Ltd
Tiling and Flooring Products
Hoefield Road, Haverhill
Suffolk CB9 8QP
www.ardex.co.uk

F Ball and Co. Ltd
Flooring membranes
Churnetside Business Park,
Station Road, Cheddleton, Leek,
Staffs ST13 7RS
www.f-ball.co.uk

H+H Celcon Ltd
Beam & Block Floors
Celcon House, Ightham,
Sevenoaks,
Kent TN15 9HZ
www.celcon.co.uk

Mitek Industries Ltd
The Alternative Joist System
Mitek House, Grazebrook Ind.
Park, Peartree Lane,
Dudley DY2 0XW

HEALTHY FLOORING

The Healthy Flooring Network
The Women's Environmental
Network
P O Box 30626, London E1 1TZ
www.healthyflooring.org

Sound Reduction Systems Ltd
Acoustic Insulation Products
Adam Street, Off Lever Street,
Bolton, BL3 2AP
www.soundreduction.co.uk

UNDERFLOOR HEATING

The Underfloor Heating
Manufacturer's Association
Belhaven House, 67 Walton Road,
East Molesey,
Surrey KT8 0DB
www.uhma.org.uk

Nu-Heat
Warm Water Underfloor Heating
Heathpark House, Devonshire
Road, Heathpark Ind. Estate,
Honiton,
Devon EX14 1SD
www.nu-heat.co.uk

EQUIPMENT PLANT HIRE

HSS Hire Shops
Group Office,
25 Willow Lane,
Mitcham,
Surrey CR4 4TS
www.hss.com

NATURAL STONE FLOORING

Hard Rock Flooring
Fleet Marston Farm, Fleet
Marston, Aylesbury,
Bucks HP18 0PZ
www.hardrockflooring.co.uk

The Delabole Slate Company
Pengelly, Delabole,
Cornwall PL33 9AZ
www.delaboleslate.com

Paris Ceramics
583 Kings Road, Chelsea,
London SW6 2EH
www.parisceramics.com

REAL WOOD FLOORING

English Timbers Ltd
1a Main Street, Kirkburn, Driffield,
East Yorkshire YO25 9DU
www.englishtimbers.co.uk

PARQUET FLOORING

Bauwerk Parkett (UK) Ltd
The Swiss Parquet Manufacturer,
Wyvols Court, Swallowfield,
Reading RG7 1WY
www.bauwerk-parkett.com

LAMINATED FLOORING

OsmoUK Floors
Ostermann & Scheiwe UK Ltd,
Osmo House,
Unit 2 Pembroke Road, Stockdale
Ind. Estate, Aylesbury,
Bucks HP20 1DB
www.osmouk.com

Kronospan Ltd
Kronoplus Flooring,
Chirk, Wrexham LL14 5NT
www.kronospan.co.uk

CORK FLOORING

Siesta Cork Tile Co.
Unit 21 Tait Road, Croydon,
Surrey CR20 2DP
www.siestacorktiles.co.uk

CARPETS

Axminster Carpets Ltd
Axminster, Devon EX13 5PQ
Tel: (01297) 33533

LIST OF SUPPLIERS

Bronte Carpets Ltd
Bankfield Mill, Greenfield Road,
Colne, Lancs BB8 9PD
www.brontecarpets.co.uk

The Carpet Foundation
MCF Complex, 60 New Road,
Kidderminster, Worcs DY10 1AQ
www.carpetfoundation.com

NATURAL FLOORING

The Alternative Flooring Company Ltd
3b Stephenson Close,
East Portway, Andover,
Hants SP10 3RU
www.alternativeflooring.com

Crucial Trading
PO Box 10469,
Birmingham B46 1WB
www.crucial-trading.com

VINYL FLOORING

The Amtico Company Ltd
Solar Park, Southside,
Solihull B90 4SH
www.amtico.com

STEEL JOIST SYSTEMS

Ward Building Components Ltd
Sherburn, Malton
North Yorkshire YO17 8PQ
www.wards.co.uk

With special thanks to:

Acova Radiators Ltd
Unit E2, Spennells Trading Estate,
Spennells Valley Road,
Kidderminster DT10 1XS
www.acova.co.uk

B&Q plc
Portswood House, 1 Hampshire
Corp. Park, Chandler's Ford,
Eastliegh, Hants SO53 3YX

Cotteswood Kitchens Ltd
Station Road, Chipping Norton,
Oxfordshire OX7 5XN
www.cotteswood.co.uk

Daryl
Alfred Road, Wallasey,
Wirral CH44 7HY
www.daryl-showers.co.uk

Doulton Bathroom Products
Cromwell Road, Cheltenham,
Glos GL52 5EP

Hammonds Furniture Ltd
Fleming Road, Harrowbrook Ind.
Estate, Hinckley,
Leics LE10 3DU

Ideal Standard
The Bathroom Works,
National Avenue,
Kingston-upon-Hull HU5 4HS
www.ideal-standard.co.uk

Jewson Ltd
Merchant House,
Binley Business Park,
Coventry CV3 2TX
www.jewson.co.uk

Magnet Ltd
Royd Ings Avenue, Keighley,
West Yorkshire BD21 4BY

Mark Wilkinson Furniture
Overton House, High Street,
Bromham SN15 2HA
www.mwf.com

MFI
For nearest store phone SCOOT
0800 192 192
www.mfi.co.uk

Shires Bathrooms
Beckside Road,
West Yorkshire BD7 2JE
www.shires-bathrooms.co.uk

Utopia Furniture Ltd
Fitted Bathroom Furniture
Springvale Business Park,
Springvale Avenue, Bilston,
Wolverhampton WV14 0QL
www.utopiagroup.com

Wickes Building Supplies Ltd
120–136 Station Road, Harrow,
Middlesex HA1 2QB

Visions
Beckside Road,
West Yorkshire BD7 2JE
www.visions-bathrooms.co.uk

INDEX

Index